A PLUME BOOK

THE LITTLE BOOK OF HEARTBREAK

Sarah McGowan

MEGHAN LASLOCKY grew up on a farm in Vermont and graduated from Middlebury College and the UC Berkeley Graduate School of Journalism. She has been dumped at least a dozen times, including on her birthday, in her own kitchen, over instant messenger, by a Willem Dafoe doppelgänger, and after moving across the country for a guy. She now lives in the Bay Area with her husband, her son, and three cats.

The

LITTLE BOOK
of HEARTBREAK

Love Gone Wrong
Through the Ages

MEGHAN LASLOCKY

A PLUME BOOK

PLUME

Published by Penguin Group

Penguin Group (USA) Inc., 375 Hudson Street, New York, New York 10014, USA •
Penguin Group (Canada), 90 Eglinton Avenue East, Suite 700, Toronto, Ontario M4P 2Y3,
Canada (a division of Pearson Penguin Canada Inc.) • Penguin Books Ltd, 80 Strand,
London WC2R 0RL, England • Penguin Ireland, 25 St Stephen's Green, Dublin 2,
Ireland (a division of Penguin Books Ltd) • Penguin Group (Australia), 707 Collins Street,
Melbourne, Victoria 3008, Australia (a division of Pearson Australia Group Pty Ltd) •
Penguin Books India Pvt Ltd, 11 Community Centre, Panchsheel Park, New Delhi – 110
017, India • Penguin Group (NZ), 67 Apollo Drive, Rosedale, Auckland 0632, New
Zealand (a division of Pearson New Zealand Ltd) • Penguin Books, Rosebank Office
Park, 181 Jan Smuts Avenue, Parktown North 2193, South Africa • Penguin China,
B7 Jaiming Center, 27 East Third Ring Road North, Chaoyang District, Beijing 100020,
China

Penguin Books Ltd., Registered Offices: 80 Strand, London WC2R 0RL, England

First published by Plume, a member of Penguin Group (USA) Inc.

First Printing, January 2013
10 9 8 7 6 5 4 3 2

Copyright © Meghan Laslocky, 2013
All rights reserved

Ⓟ REGISTERED TRADEMARK—MARCA REGISTRADA

LIBRARY OF CONGRESS CATALOGING-IN-PUBLICATION DATA

Laslocky, Meghan.
  The little book of heartbreak : love gone wrong through the ages / Meghan Laslocky.
    p. cm.
  Includes bibliographical references and index.
  ISBN 978-0-452-29832-3
  1. Couples.   2. Love.   3. Separation (Psychology)   4. Adjustment (Psychology)
I. Title.
  HQ801.L313 2012
  306.7—dc23

                                                              2012018688

Printed in the United States of America
Set in Granjon LT Std
Designed by Victoria Hartman

PUBLISHER'S NOTE
While the author has made every effort to provide accurate telephone numbers, Internet
addresses, and other contact information at the time of publication, neither the publisher
nor the author assumes any responsibility for errors, or for changes that occur after
publication. Further, publisher does not have any control over and does not assume any
responsibility for author or third-party Web sites or their content.

BOOKS ARE AVAILABLE AT QUANTITY DISCOUNTS WHEN USED TO PROMOTE PRODUCTS OR
SERVICES. FOR INFORMATION PLEASE WRITE TO PREMIUM MARKETING DIVISION, PENGUIN
GROUP (USA) INC., 375 HUDSON STREET, NEW YORK, NEW YORK 10014.

For Brandon and Henry,

who shooed heartbreak away

Contents

Acknowledgments

LITTLE AS IT IS, this book was many years in the making—or at least the thinking. So many people have helped me along the way with their support, expertise, personal experience, and good old-fashioned words of wisdom, and without them *The Little Book of Heartbreak* would still be an unwieldy pile of notes in a little-visited folder on my desktop.

First of all, many thanks to my agent, Lindsay Edgecombe of Levine Greenberg Literary Agency, who not only bravely requested a brain dump and got one but could see in that vast mess the kernel of an idea that became *The Little Book of Heartbreak*. Then to my editor, Kate Napolitano, I owe eternal gratitude for understanding from the get-go what this book should be, as well as for her incisive and exacting edits, enthusiasm, and patience. Over the course of the months it took to write this book, Lindsay, Kate, and I became a triumvirate, and surely no three women have ever thought harder about the conundrum that is love gone wrong.

My husband and son, Brandon and Henry Sprague, put up with months of my crankiness and a chronic shortage of clean underwear, and for that I cannot say thank you enough. My sister, Jenna Laslocky, and my parents, Russell and Fleur Laslocky, were patient and supportive during the many interactions when I was vague and distracted (probably because I was typing or reading while I talked), as were my in-laws, the ever-lovely Douglas Sprague and Natalie Forrest.

For their expertise in various and sundry areas that are obscure to most mere mortals, I thank Zoltán Kövecses, Ethan Kross, Phillip Shaver, Eric Jager, Art Aron, Geoff MacDonald, Poppy Siahaan, Marc Ettlinger, Silvia Evangelisti, and Xiaobing Tang.

Without Adam Hochschild and Deirdre English of the UC Berkeley Graduate School of Journalism, I'm not sure where I would be (but I'm pretty sure it wouldn't involve having my first book under my belt). Ditto for my brilliant, wry, and wise therapist, Dr. Mitchell Wilson, whom I first began to see years ago when I was a puddle of heartbreak and under whose watch I have become (I hope!) the person I'm supposed to be.

My friend and fellow debut author Stephanie V. W. Lucianovic deserves a special shout-out, not only for immediately understanding the basic idea of the book and going to bat for it but for the many times when she picked up the phone on the first ring. Writing a book is a long and lonely process, and there were many moments when it felt as if Stephanie was the only one who could really hold my hand.

Then thank you to my many wonderful other friends, whether they cheered me on when I was overwhelmed, shared tidbits from their own heartbreak histories, or turned me on to their favorite song about love gone wrong: Kae Sharpe Drasin, Diane Lafleur, Leonore Reiser, Cerissa Tanner, Frankie Dunleavy Yeaton, Ben Charny, Colleen Wilson, Victoria Mills, Jean Messier, Jennifer Harrison, Debbie Zambetti, Jocelyn Lamm Startz, Britty Shaw, Grace Jeffers, Alisa Weinstein, Daniella Korotzer, Sara Eichner, and Tiffany Shackelford.

Finally, while I never thought I'd issue a thank-you to the men who shotgunned pain under my breastbone, here we are, all these years later. This one's for you, boys.

Introduction

O<small>N A BRILLIANT</small> September day many years ago, a man in an aged butter-yellow Volvo backed out of my driveway and out of my life. Ours was a short-lived romance, but a passionate one that had smacked of fate. I stood helpless on the gravel, crying as I watched him barrel away in reverse, his head turned from me toward his rear window, his arm wrapped over the passenger seat.

Flash forward a minute: the sun still high in the sky over a hayfield outside my kitchen window and artifacts of communion transformed into midden—on the table the bottle of wine and the bar of chocolate he'd inexplicably brought (who brings gifts to a breakup?); the scraps of the dinner I'd started (salad, kabobs) scattered across the counter. And then there was the pain—a piercing crush in my chest so acute that I wanted to displace it, to redirect it anywhere.

Months later tears could still spill into the dishwater and gasps of grief could suddenly unhinge a set of sit-ups. Now, over fifteen years and several more heartbreaks later, a photo of this man, excavated online, still makes my heart rev—with lust, confusion, sadness, and, I suspect, fear. Even though the immediate pain in my chest triggered by that moment has long since departed, I can still feel its echo in my body when I stop and allow myself to "go there."

And to this day a rare butter-yellow Volvo spied on the freeway remains my heart's madeleine.

This book is about romantic heartbreak, the subset of grief and the pain that barnacles the human chest and soul. In it I attempt to weave together the disparate threads that collectively inform and shape our notion and experience of heartbreak, drawing from history, culture, science, literature, and art. From the terrible story of the twelfth-century French lovers Abelard and Heloise to the physiological dance between brain and body that explains why lost love hurts; from ancient Greek love magic, which is at moments shockingly violent and at others reassuringly familiar to the reasons the film *Eternal Sunshine of the Spotless Mind* resonates in its devastating portrayal of modern love, each section of *The Little Book of Heartbreak* is meant to make you ponder. Sometimes you might not be sure whether to laugh or cry, so ridiculous are some moments (just wait for the shenanigans of painter Oskar Kokoschka and the antics of Lady Caroline Lamb) and so tragic are others (keep tissues on hand for the story of composer Johannes Brahms and pianist Clara Schumann). There are moments when you'll shake your head in disbelief, others when you'll nod with sympathy.

The Little Book of Heartbreak is by no means encyclopedic, and it is deliberately nomadic. I wrote about what captured my imagination, whether it was a messy annulment case from Renaissance Florence or the bellicose ways of Norman Mailer. I wanted to shed light on the lives of others, which might seem distant but illustrate the universal ways in which we cope with love gone wrong— whether that means hitting the bottle too hard or penning a letter to an ex that, quite frankly, reads as if you've utterly lost it. My research amounted to a tour through medical journals, biographies, ethnographies, medieval scholarly chronicles, and even handbooks translated from ancient Greek, and all the while I felt like the happiest dog in the world, sniffing at everything on a long walk in the woods.

The Little Book of Heartbreak is meant to entertain, but it is also meant to soothe, distract, heal, and engross readers who are themselves in the throes of romantic disappointment. In my darkest times, "bibliotherapy" has saved me; reading about and intellectualizing my suffering strangely helped to distract me from it. To books I owe my life.

Reading a book is in some ways a metaphor for healing. Progress is incremental, each fresh page builds on the one before it, each page creeps into our souls. Read *The Little Book of Heartbreak* and weep, and may every page make you feel a tiny bit better.

· I ·

HISTORY

THE OLDER I get, the more irked I become that time travel is not an option. Nothing would make me happier than stocking up on olives in the Roman Forum, introducing Queen Elizabeth I to vodka gimlets, flirting with a caveman, catching a Dickens reading in St. James's Hall, or hand-feeding a brachiosaur. These impossible and perhaps relatively simple adventures are easy to imagine.

But when it comes to imagining *love* in times gone by, I am often flummoxed. Don't we all walk around with the assumption that every culture and every era before the 1960s was infinitely more formal and less intimate than our own? Something makes us think that until about fifty years ago, no one screwed with abandon, had lovers' spats, suffered through silent treatments, or lazed in pillow talk—as if we invented the accoutrements of love along with the Pill and all previous eras were starved of it.

Certainly there may be something to the notion that for our ancestors love was a less complex experience, and as the historian Stephanie Coontz points out, "People have always loved a love story. But for most of the past our ancestors did not try to live in one." One couldn't be too picky or dramatic when his home was a village with only a handful of partners to choose from and when what most people needed was a work partner, not a soul mate.

Love as many of us pursue and enjoy it now—openly and single-mindedly, unfettered by dangerous crises like starvation and disease—is a modern luxury.

But it's also the case that love itself, as in the biochemical alchemy that occurs in our brains, has been more or less the same in humans for millennia. Spend some time going down the convoluted rabbit hole of history and trust me, heartbreak still emerges from the rubble of passion, repression, and punishment.

East and West: Love Across the Globe

FIRST LET'S DO a crash course on how love unfolded in the West (in Europe and its immediate affiliates) and in China—two traditions that are in many ways about as different as can be but have arrived, for the time being at any rate, in much the same place.

Fitzwilliam Darcy: Spawned by the Enlightenment

In the West, down through recorded history, the most enduring love stories were cautionary tales. Romantic love was dangerous. When Aeneas left Dido, she offed herself on top of a funeral pyre; Romeo guzzled poison, and Juliet plunged a dagger into her own heart; Abelard was castrated and Heloise was cloistered; and so on and so on. Western literature shook a finger at the populace: Passionate love, it warned, ends in disaster—shame, suicide, banishment, or dismemberment.

The passionate parts of these stories surely offered vicarious thrills to the loveless masses, while the ruinous parts kept them in check: *Don't disrupt the social order. You are just a tiny part of a greater, unknowable scheme.* In eras when property was amassed and allegiances were forged largely through arranged marriages and associated dowries, this made sense. Love and lust could throw a mighty kink into Daddy's plans.

But around 1500, things started to change, thanks to the cultural transformations spawned by the Age of Discovery, the Renaissance, the Enlightenment, and the scientific and industrial revolutions. People realized that they were individuals and that as individuals they had the right to be happy. And love could, in theory, make a person happy. Aldous Huxley, the British writer and intellectual, placed the tipping point in the eighteenth century, with the rise of Romanticism, a movement he described as a "cult of passion for passion's sake."

Some take this argument a step further, maintaining that until the Enlightenment and the Age of Reason, religion had a monopoly on men's passion, but as people became less religious, they found similar comfort and stimulation in romantic love. In essence, romantic love replaced organized religion for many people. By 1800, marrying for love—and both looking for and waiting for it—was a noble aspiration, as some of the most lasting stories of the period suggest: Super-rich Fitzwilliam Darcy married middle-class Elizabeth Bennet for love; Fairfax Rochester defied convention by falling in love with and ultimately marrying his governess, the orphan Jane Eyre; and even crème de la crème rulers like Victoria and Albert were passionately in love. The disastrous ends faced by real-life Heloise and Abelard and fictional Romeo and Juliet are in some ways quaint reminders of how far we've come, while Darcy still makes us weak in the knees.

Meanwhile, Across the Globe . . .

In comparison, love unfolded very differently in the home of one of the other largest and most influential cultures of the world,

China. Chinese historians maintain that for the first four thousand years of its recorded history (about 3000 BC to AD 1000), romantic love—and its close associate, sex—was viewed as a good thing—healthy, virtuous, and joyful. And not just boy-girl love. Homosexuality was accepted and even widely practiced among the upper classes, and lesbian relationships were applauded in literature and art.

But the rise of the Song dynasty, around AD 1000, marked a shift in attitudes toward love and sex, attitudes that still linger in China. As neo-Confucians gained political and religious power, their far more restrictive attitudes regarding love and sex took hold. A classic story from that era, "The Jade Goddess," is a variation of *Romeo and Juliet*, complete with the message that love is dangerous—boy meets girl, boy and girl elope, boy and girl are discovered, boy is beaten and banished, girl is beaten and buried alive. Mainstream naughty art or literature, as well as the displays of affection among unmarried couples that had once been socially accepted, went poof and were replaced with stuffiness and prudishness.

As modernity and Western influences crept into China in the early twentieth century, change was dramatic, particularly in Shanghai, a city whose population jumped from fifty thousand to a million between 1850 and 1900 thanks to the British appetite for opium. By the late 1920s, Shanghai was the "Paris of the Orient," known for louche behavior that even a Parisian could admire. But this experimentation lasted a mere moment, relatively speaking. With communism's triumph over the mainland in 1949, the Chinese were faced with the conundrum of how to reconcile modern freedoms, including freedom to marry whomever you chose, with the edict that people should love their country above all else. These contradictions intensified during the Cultural Revolution; the collective economy meant that more women joined the labor force, causing more mobility and social interaction, which in turn gave people the chance to better exercise free choice when it came to marriage. Despite these seeming advancements, romantic love was still condemned in favor of the greater good. In the fifties and sixties, the ideal Chinese husband was part of the establishment, either as a worker for the railway system or in a military factory, not an object of sexual passion.

Then, under Deng Xiaoping, much of this was reversed. The Cultural Revolution itself was denounced, and in 1980 the Marriage Law was revised to state specifically that marriage should be based on mutual affection. Needless to say, under more liberal policies the Chinese "bounced back" quickly. A few years ago, the quite possibly embellished story of a couple who fell passionately in love and eloped more than fifty years before, lived in seclusion in a cave, and ate grass and roots in order to live together in peace became all the rage on online news sites. Readers swooned over the fact that the man had carved six thousand steps into the mountainside so that his beloved wife could get up and down the mountain the few times she left their home. And while conservative Chinese might frown in dismay, sex has crept back into the spotlight, too: Racy chick lit is available, popular newspapers coach readers on how to bring on "high tide" (orgasm), and a Chinese Sexual Culture Museum in Shanghai boasts a collection of more than four thousand historical artifacts, including a wince-inducing donkey saddle equipped with a wooden dildo (once used to punish adulterous women with an extra-special ride through town). But more to the point, unmarried couples in China now hold hands in the streets, and, more and more, love and romance are considered important components to marriage. Unlike the way it was a hundred or even fifty years ago, a romance that leads to marriage in Beijing is likely to follow more or less the same general path as one in New York, London, or Rome.

Unfinished Business:
The Tragedy of Heloise and Abelard

To THE MODERN EYE, human figures in medieval art look like paper dolls, one-dimensional and expressionless, slapped against scenes of religion and war. A viewer is apt to walk away with the impression that people of the era were as wooden and lacking in self-awareness as contemporary depictions suggest.

But spend some time examining the minute stitches of the story of Abelard and Heloise—arguably history's most dramatic, detailed, and poignant love story, picked apart ad nauseam by scholars for centuries—and the anguish is as fresh as your morning bagel.

City of Light, 1115

Picture Paris around 1115: Gothic architecture had yet to make its debut, and much of the city was still in ruins from a brutal sacking by the Vikings several centuries earlier. Paris's heart and soul was the Île de la Cité, home to hundreds of scholars and clerics, students and government officials. The streets were no doubt contradictory in nature: noisy and filled with the rowdy carousing of any university town, but also darkened by the rise of monasticism.

At the academic community's epicenter was thirty-six-year-old Peter Abelard, a brilliant philosopher who specialized in logic and coined the term "theology," or "God logic." Championing reason over superstition was dangerous work in a deeply religious society, where an academic quibble could quickly escalate into an accusation of heresy, but Abelard was a gifted teacher and a bulldog when arguing. He was ferociously smart, eloquent, handsome, charismatic, and funny, but also cocky, arrogant, pugnacious, and ruthlessly ambitious. Everyone in Paris, and everyone in academe across Europe, knew exactly who Peter Abelard was. If twelfth-century Europe had had *People* magazine, Peter Abelard would have been a cover boy.

Into Abelard's environment of intellectual debate and rock-star fame entered Heloise, who had been raised at a convent called Argenteuil, just outside Paris, and who, like him, was a brilliant intellectual but an even rarer bird, because she was a well-educated *woman*. While her field was more literature than philosophy, it stands to reason that the smart, pretty Heloise (whose exact age is unclear but was between seventeen and twenty-two in 1115) left Argenteuil and moved to her uncle's house in Notre Dame in part to bask in the glow of Abelard. One can imagine that the moment they set eyes on each other, perhaps crossing paths in a crowded street, each knew who the other was and the attraction was immediate and electric.

Abelard moved quickly by volunteering to be Heloise's private tutor. Heloise's uncle, a cleric named Fulbert, was so thrilled by the prospect of the celebrity scholar teaching his niece that he offered Abelard lodging in their home as well. Given that Abelard aimed to seduce Heloise, sleeping under the same roof with her was almost too good to be true from his point of view.

What Abelard, the arrogant master of logic, might not have anticipated was that he would fall wildly in love with Heloise and she with him. He wrote her love songs, they traded notes, and presumably they sneaked around at night into each other's bed. Abelard's teaching began to suffer, and their affair was more or less an open secret—after all, his love songs to her were in the public domain. It seemed that everyone knew except the willfully ignorant Fulbert. Whatever Fulbert's reasons for being so dense, when he walked in on them in flagrante delicto, the jig was up. Fulbert threw Abelard out—a turn of events that was naturally the buzz of Paris. If Île de la Cité was medieval France's Hogwarts, it was as if Gilderoy had been busted with an age-of-consent Hermione. Worse, before long it was clear that Île de la Cité's Hermione was knocked up.

A Bun in the Oven

Abelard wasted no time: He disguised his pregnant girlfriend in a nun's habit and whisked her off to his family's home in Brittany, nearly three hundred miles to the southwest. Heloise stayed there for the rest of her pregnancy and gave birth to a son. Inspired by a handheld model of the heavens, she named him Astrolabe—perhaps the medieval equivalent of Shiloh Nouvel Jolie-Pitt or Moon Unit Zappa.

Now, with an illegitimate child and a career path that *theoretically* demanded celibacy, Abelard was in a pickle. On one hand he needed to appease Fulbert in order to protect his family; on the other, marriage would compromise the next step in his brilliant career. In what must have been a tense meeting, Fulbert and Abelard came to an agreement: Abelard and Heloise would marry in secret. It appeared that Abelard would have his cake and eat it, too.

Heloise returned to Paris, and marry in secret they did, at dawn in a church after an all-nighter of prayer, in the presence of Fulbert

and a few other witnesses. Abelard and Heloise settled into a routine of seeing each other rarely and discreetly. But back at Fulbert's
house, Heloise and Fulbert fought. It was in Fulbert's interest to
leak the truth—that his niece was no longer a whore, his grand-
nephew was no longer a bastard—but Heloise, for reasons of her
own, had reservations about the marriage in the first place and did
not want the world to know.

Now comes the point in the story that, with twenty-twenty
hindsight, they must have seen as their tragic tipping point: Abelard spirited Heloise away yet again, this time to Argenteuil, the
convent where she'd grown up. It was familiar turf, but, even better, it was a mere seven miles from the center of Paris—in short, a
booty call away. Who knows what Abelard's reasoning was here.
Did he want to protect Heloise from Fulbert's wrath? Was it an
attempt to hush up gossip? Did he think he'd have more unfettered
access to her at the convent than he did at Fulbert's house? Or, as
one scholar has suggested, was his ardor cooling, as it does for
many of us a few years into a relationship?

Snip, Snip, Vow, Vow

Fulbert assumed that by moving Heloise to a convent, Abelard was
signaling his intent to divorce her. Not bothering to confirm his sus-
picion, he took drastic action by hiring a band of thugs to break into
Abelard's lodgings and castrate him in his bed. In that, they succeded.

In the pitch-black mayhem that must have ensued, revenge was
swift: Two of the assailants were immediately castrated and
blinded on the spot, likely by servants from the household where
Abelard was staying, while doctors were doubtless called as Abelard risked going into shock. Imagine the scene: violent shouts,
men stumbling through the streets maimed and bloody. A family

feud had suddenly gone postal, all within the confines of a religious precinct.

For weeks afterward the maiming of Abelard was the talk of Paris. The city's golden boy had been taken down in the worst imaginable way; he was suddenly more famous for what he didn't have than for what he did have. Surely a good quantity of beer and wine was consumed as the residents of Paris teased out the motive and the meaning of the act. Was Fulbert seized by rage over loss of control of his beloved Heloise, or was he motivated by paternal shame or, worse, by sexual jealousy? Whatever the case, castrating his niece's husband wasn't just about wounding and humiliating him. It was also about the long-term effects it would have on his very being, about making sure Abelard would never be sexy again.

Abelard might have lost his cojones, but he was still the husband and therefore still the boss. One logical solution at the time would have been to have the marriage annulled so at least Heloise could move on with her life, but Abelard decided that the best course of action was for the two of them to take vows. Heloise would officially become a nun at Argenteuil, and he would follow by becoming a monk at Saint-Denis, one of the most prestigious monasteries in France. Just before taking her vows, with Abelard present as a witness, Heloise dramatically burst out with a lament from an ancient Latin text in which a woman blames her husband's loss in battle on herself, the key line of which is "The guilt was mine for this disastrous marriage!"

Abelard Airs His Laundry

One would think that the pain would have peaked there, but no, as heartbreak often does, it lurked for years, only to make the most extraordinary revival much later.

Years passed. Abelard became something of an itinerant scholar, moving from place to place, attracting students, pissing off superiors, and dealing with what we would now classify as "hate mail." (According to James Burge, author of *Heloise and Abelard: A Twelfth-Century Love Story*, one former teacher memorably refused to call him Peter because it was a masculine name and Abelard was no longer a man—in other words, the man's reasoning was that "if your name is Peter but you don't have a peter, then you're not a man and you're not Peter either.")

Heloise meanwhile seemingly kept her nose to the grindstone with prayer, devotion, and administrative skill. She rose to become prioress—that's second-in-command—at Argenteuil. But by the time Heloise was in her early thirties, church politics rendered her and the other nuns homeless. Abelard came to their rescue and offered a property called La Paracléte, where he'd been a hermit several years earlier, as their new home.

Heloise was named abbess of La Paracléte, and because we know that Abelard visited the rustic site to preach, we have to assume that they saw each other. Perhaps they walked the grounds together, making plans to upgrade the domestic structures to better house a group of women, and one imagines that Heloise being Heloise—deeply self-aware, outspoken, passionate—brought up their shared history and that Abelard, ever the logician and egomaniac, a bit dense about people's feelings—tried to shove it under the rug. Keep in mind as well that by this time the physical effects of his castration well over a decade earlier would have taken their toll; he likely would have become plump and womanish, with hips and maybe even breasts, and his beard may have thinned. For Heloise to see the man with whom she'd shared such a profoundly erotic connection so physically transformed must have been very painful. Whatever the case, what happens next suggests that their communication during this time was appropriate to him but unsatisfying for her.

By 1132, Abelard was abbot of Saint-Gildas-de-Rhuys, a mon-astery in Brittany known for its dissolute and often married monks who so hated him for his bad management skills that they repeat-edly tried to poison him with the sacramental wine. Whether it truly was a private letter or was intended to underpin a PR cam-paign, or whether all along he meant it as a sort of "bcc: Heloise" is unclear, but Abelard penned a memoir, later called *Historia Calamitatum* (History of My Calamities) by scholars, in the form of a letter of consolation to an unnamed close friend—a sort of "You think your life sucks? Listen to mine" diatribe.

"History of My Calamities" reads like the howl of a man in the midst of a midlife crisis. Abelard devoted considerable space to re-counting intimate details of his relationship with Heloise, saying how she was a "lamb" to his "ravening wolf" and what an easy target she was. Not only that, but he arrogantly stated, according to a translation of their correspondence by the scholar William Levitan, that "I was famous myself at that time, young, and exceptionally good-looking, and could not imagine that any woman I thought worthy of my love would turn me down. But I thought this particular girl would be more likely to give in because of her knowledge and love of letters." Other doozies included allu-sions to their appetite for kinky sex ("if love could find something novel or strange, we tried that too"), how they shagged with aban-don on feast days, and how he caressed her breasts while they worked in her uncle's study. In short, one gets the sense that young Abelard was the type who, if he lived now, would have sexted He-loise a picture of himself and assumed he was doing her a very large favor.

But Abelard also maintained in "History of My Calamities" that the slice-and-dice punishment for his sins was just, and he went to great pains to explain that Heloise objected to getting mar-ried in the first place. She believed, he wrote, that even a secret marriage would never appease her uncle (she was right), and that marriage and family life would, quite simply, bring Abelard down. Heloise had argued that one cannot be both a philosopher and a husband; his career should take precedence. He recounted that she said he had been made for all of mankind to enjoy rather than to be limited as the property of one woman. She suggested, moreover, that they enjoy "love freely offered" rather than that forced by marriage, that they see each other joyfully and rarely.

Heloise, in short, would not be the first or the last person to suggest that marriage just might ruin a good thing. By his telling, she thought that enslaving the most brilliant man of his generation would inevitably end in disaster. "There is only one thing left for us," he remembered her saying, "that in our utter ruin the pain to come will be no less than the love that has gone before."

Although social networks then didn't operate at the lightning speed they do now, his memoir quickly went viral. While it's always a shock to see oneself referred to in the third person, imagine Heloise's horror when she saw intimate details of her life splayed on parchment for all the world to see. And not only that, but he was dismissive of her—he'd reduced a passion that was intellectual as much as it was sexual to mere lust. It was, one imagines, not so unlike a present-day celebrity writing a tell-all with sordid details about an equally famous ex. The "history of his calamities" must have stunned and hurt her beyond measure.

Hints from Heloise

By now it was twelve years since their separation, and Heloise appears to have wasted little time in drafting a private response to Abelard's memoir. From there a series of letters between them unfolded, letters that are simply astounding in their emotional rigor.

As William Levitan said of the extant correspondence between Heloise and Abelard, "Few works in Latin literature approach the urgency of these letters, their poignancy, or sense of personal drama. Few project more vivid, complex voices. Few works are more scandalous and frank."

Numerous translations of the letters are out there (and they are worth reading), but for our purposes the most compelling bits are not just the salacious details that surface (good God, they even had sex in the communal dining room when he visited her at Argenteuil!) but the fact that a decade after the abrupt and violent end of their affair Heloise was still racked by a potent combination of rage and desire.

♥ Letters Between Monks and Nuns

Monks and nuns were often the best-educated individuals in medieval Europe—and, presumably, very sexually frustrated. In *The Book of the Heart*, medievalist Eric Jager suggests that it's hard to determine if the trading of sexy letters between men and women of the cloth was intellectual entertainment akin to a game of chess, evidence of brazen sexual play, or was more a manifestation of spiritual rather than sexual or romantic hunger. But for modern readers, it's hard to imagine letters like this one, from a young Constance of Angers to the much older Baudri of Bourgueil and translated by Peter Dronke, as anything but candidly erotic:

> I put [your] letter under my left breast—
> they say that's nearest the heart . . .
> At last, weary, I tried to get to sleep,
> but love that has been wakened knows no night . . .
> I lay asleep—no, sleepless—because the page you wrote,
> though lying on my breast, had set my womb on fire.

For men and women who had forsaken sex, playing at having sexual relationships must have been delightfully subversive.

How dare he, she ventured in her first volley, not only publicize their intimate history but also describe it in such a way that trivializes their connection (or at least his feelings for her). He might think from outward appearances that she's doing just fine, she says, but really, she's a mess and desperately needs support from her husband. Abelard responds that, well, it never occurred to him that she needed propping up (she really is so very pious, and all she needs is God!) and the only important thing is that she pray for him.

No doubt extremely frustrated by his response, Heloise takes it up a notch in her second letter to him: Thanks to him, she writes, she is the unhappiest and unluckiest of all women, while he, having already paid the price for their sins, can in essence rest on his laurels. But even more fascinatingly, and poignantly, she confesses to him that all these years later, memories of their liaison make her seethe with desire. Even when she's supposed to be praying during Holy Mass, she's reliving the tiniest moments of their sex life. Sometimes it gets so bad that she bursts out with a thought or a movement that betrays what she's really thinking about. Her sexual fantasies are so overpowering, she writes, that as a nun, much less a leader of nuns, she is a massive hypocrite. In essence, she says, "Pious, schmious. You were and are the love of my life, I'd take approval from you over God any day, I'll never get laid again, and I'll surely go to hell for all of it."

Ultimately they reached an impasse: Abelard was unwavering in his argument that God saved them by punishing them for their many sins (he even had the nerve to go after her for having worn a nun's habit while she was pregnant and he was whisking her off to Brittany), and that she really needed to just get over it and accept the fact that this was all God's plan. "Cry for your savior, not your seducer," he basically tells her, "and channel all that lust into your work." (One could argue that by making her go into a convent "freely at [his] command," he more or less attempted to lop off her sexuality just as his had been. Problem was his testosterone, and therefore his sex drive, had been shut down, while she retained all the usual appetites of a healthy thirtysomething woman.)

Getting him to "get it" must have felt to her like soliciting the proverbial blood from a stone. Finally she responded that although she'd always be unhappy about the situation, she'd at least attempt to shut up about their personal history and focus instead on a correspondence with him that was restricted to theology and the administration of La Paracléte. Even then, however, she managed to slide in little bits that are clearly meant to remind him of the past, like when she asks his advice on what sort of underclothes menstruating nuns should wear (read: Despite your piety, my man, you know perfectly well what a vagina is and what it does once a month).

All these centuries later, once you get past the conventions of medieval letter writing I think it's the familiarity of the mismatch between Heloise's and Abelard's points of view in their letters that is so touching, and so timeless. She demands more intimacy and wants to set the record straight, while his perspective from what we would now call "closure" is resolute. In short, it reads remarkably like the transcript from a couples-therapy session. I'm not a particular believer in the afterlife, but I sure hope that if there is one, Heloise has once again loved with abandon.

Abelard died in 1142, and as he requested in his letters to Heloise, he was buried at La Paracléte. When Heloise died in her late sixties, she was buried next to him. Their remains were moved a whopping five times after that, until they were finally interred in 1817 in what was then a new, and unpopular, cemetery outside Paris called Père Lachaise. Once dirt was turned at Père Lachaise for Abelard and Heloise, being buried there became all the rage: Frédéric Chopin, Oscar Wilde, Jim Morrison, Colette, Eugène Delacroix, and Marcel Proust are just a few of the hallowed souls laid to rest there.

♥ Etch A Sketch, Twelfth-Century Style

In 1980 a British scholar named Constant Mews stumbled across the holy grail of French letters: the daily love notes passed between Abelard and Heloise in the early stages of their affair.

To me the most delightful aspect of this find is not so much the content of the letters but the manner in which they were exchanged, as James Burge details in his wonderful book *Heloise and Abelard: A Twelfth-Century Love Story*. In those days if two people needed to exchange short messages, they used notebooks made of wax tablets. One person would inscribe a message in the wax with a stylus and dispatch it via a servant; the recipient would then read it, erase the message by warming the wax and pressing it smooth, and then inscribe a response and send the tablet back. Servants didn't read Latin, so the exchange could be exquisitely private. Heloise likely recorded each of their letters dutifully on parchment so that she could savor them later— just the way, today, we might scroll through old e-mails or text messages to relive the unfolding intimacies of a relationship. Sometime in the fifteenth century, a monk found fragments of what she'd copied and quietly compiled them in a handbook on letter writing; there they waited for centuries before they were discovered.

The Mystery of Courtly Love

In 1883 a French writer and scholar by the name of Gaston Paris coined the term "courtly love" to describe a medieval phenomenon in which knights proclaimed undying love for married aristocratic ladies and subjected themselves to various tests to prove their ardor. Common courtly-love clichés include that of the young knight heading into a joust with a ribbon from his lady tied to his lance, as well as knights mooning around noble halls writing love songs and dedicating them to a particular woman. The whole point of courtly love was that it was unrequited and elevating. The nobility of it was in the longing, and consummation was *theoretically* verboten. Courtly love, if it existed, codified heartbreak.

Wrapping one's mind around medieval courtly love is, for a modern person, an acrobatic task. First of all, it's hard to imagine a scenario in which a man would declare his love for a married woman of superior social standing—like his lord's wife—and then make a point of publicly moping about when she said no. (The only modern equivalent I can think of would be if a midlevel manager declared his love for the CEO's wife, sailed into tough meetings with her Hermès scarf wrapped around his arm, and then cried to the crowd around the watercooler about how she didn't love him back.) I'm all for cultural relativism, but no matter what the context, the code of courtly love strikes me as ridiculous. There are some things men just don't do, and one of them is openly pursue the boss's wife. Moreover, it's pretty tough to reconcile the idea of obsessing over another man's wife with medieval Christianity. After all, it would seem a bit contradictory for a knight to spend a few years on a Crusade defending Christianity only to come home and be expected to covet another man's wife.

In theory a knight's love for a lady might unfold in the following stages:

1. Knight attempts to attract lady's attention via stolen glances, perhaps from across a crowded banquet hall.
2. Knight circles lady like a shark, perhaps by attending court just a little more often.
3. Knight declares, "I love you," perhaps from behind a curtain or in a dark corner.
4. Lady replies, "No, no, no! I'm so very married and so very devout!"
5. Knight falls on knees, says, "I don't care! I'll love you forever! I'll do anything to win your heart!"
6. Knight says he just might die if lady doesn't return his love.
7. Knight gets a hold of ribbon from lady, ties it to his lance, and proceeds to win a jousting tournament (bonus points for non-life-threatening injuries sustained).
8. Lady is at last persuaded, sleeps with or at least kisses knight.
9. Knight and lady enjoy the thrill of avoiding detection.

If the secrecy, the cries of "no, no, no," the slavish devotion, the injuries sustained, and the restraint ring any bells, it just might be because courtly love was on some level a precursor to what we would now call BDSM (bondage/discipline/sadism/masochism).

Among those who have studied it, however, there are sharp divides over courtly love. Some think it existed as described, others that it was more of a ruse used to cover, justify, or even celebrate adultery as the highest form of love in a milieu where marriages were arranged and loveless. But when it comes to how it reflects on women's history, interpretations of it fall into two categories: (1) that it did indeed exist and was in essence a sexual revolution in which women radically turned the tables on men; and (2) that it never really existed and that anyone who believes it did, much less that it was a real social revolution, is suffering from an acute bout of wishful thinking. And both sides rely on evidence from the life of the formidable Eleanor of Aquitaine.

The believers maintain that Eleanor of Aquitaine, one of the most powerful women in Europe, had a bit of a problem on her hands when she maintained a court in Poitiers while her second husband, Henry II, was off attending to his own affairs. Namely, young men were returning from the Crusades and wreaking havoc; they were a boisterous, bellicose lot (many were poor, landless younger sons of lords) bent on jousting, gambling, and getting laid. Eleanor needed to come up with some way of controlling these troublemakers, and she saw an opportunity to kill two birds with one stone: teach them how to behave civilly *and* elevate women to their rightful status as superior to men. So she enlisted her daughter, Marie of Champagne, and together they founded what one might call an academy. According to this interpretation, Marie then hired a fellow by the name of Andreas Capellanus ("Andrew the Chaplain") to ghostwrite a treatise called *Tractus de Amore et de Amoris Remedia* (*Treatise on Love and the Remedies of Love*, commonly referred to among historians as *de Amore*), which outlined a code of love that taught men not just to be polite and chaste but to obey women. Key in this document were references to something called "courts of love," in which women of Eleanor's court—perhaps sixty or more, seated on a raised dais—supposedly heard "cases" related to the nature of love and debated the finer points of how romantic love was to be conducted. The most famous of these cases was one in which the question "Can real love exist between a husband and wife?" was posed and Marie, backed by her mother, determined that love cannot "exert its powers between two people who are married to each other." That would mean that illicit but proscribed, ritualized love between a lady and a knight, not marriage, was the place for passion.

As the thinking goes, Eleanor was so powerful and her court was so fashionable that thanks to *de Amore*, courtly love spread like wildfire across Europe. Marion Meade, one of the proponents of the theory that courtly love transformed upper-class women from silent vessels into power brokers, wrote in her popular biography of Eleanor of Aquitaine that with courtly love Eleanor aimed to create a new world order in which an aristocratic woman "is supreme, a goddess to be approached with reverence, and the man is her property. No chattel to be bought and sold and traded at man's whim, no sex object to be seduced and raped against her will, she holds the power to accept or reject a man, and, however difficult the trials she sets for him, he must treat her with respect and humility."

The many critics of this interpretation would say that it is more or less feminist claptrap, and it's no coincidence that its popularity spiked in the 1970s and that it was perpetuated by an author (Meade) who isn't a trained historian. In *Eleanor of Aquitaine: Queen and Legend*, published in 1996, the medieval scholar D.D.R. Owen gently suggests that Eleanor's contributions to courtly love are overstated and that the courts of love described in *de Amore* quite possibly never even existed.

In 2009's *Eleanor of Aquitaine: Queen of France, Queen of England*, the historian Ralph V. Turner suggests that maybe courtly love was, on different levels and for different people, no more than fantasy. For Eleanor it might have been a power fantasy; for ladies in loveless marriages it might have been a way to dream about a union with someone they actually loved and at least get in a good flirt in the process; and for knights who were landless it was a way to at least dream about a better life. Moreover, while plenty of historians before him point to the scant evidence that courtly love ever existed (there are, for example, no records of the courts of love and no records of specific historical cases of a knight pursuing a lady of higher rank), Turner goes so far as to suggest that *de Amore*—really the document that much of courtly love hinges on—just might have been satire written independently by Andreas Capellanus to mock the idea of courtly love and possibly even Eleanor herself.

In other words, there might be a perfectly good reason it's so hard for us to get our minds around courtly love, and that reason is that for medieval people courtly love wasn't an actual practice but a collective fantasy and a ruse. While it might be a stretch to say that in its time courtly love was a joke, that sure would explain why it's so hard to comprehend. In which case the joke is definitely on us.

He Said, She Said in
Fifteenth-Century Florence

I‌F J‌U‌D‌G‌E J‌U‌D‌Y had presided over a case we'll call *Nucci v. della Casa*, back in fifteenth-century Florence, I'm pretty sure she would have uttered one of her classic lines to Signor della Casa: "Don't pee on my leg and tell me it's raining." At issue was whether the defendant, Giovanni di Ser Lodovico della Casa, a nobleman, was married to the plaintiff, Lusanna Nucci, the beautiful widow of a cloth maker. If he was, as the plaintiff and her family claimed, then he was not only her rightful husband but a bigamist.

Giovanni and Lusanna's story is not well-known, but it definitely packs a satisfying punch for those of us who are fans of courtroom dramas, messy love stories, or anything Florentine. As detailed in Gene Brucker's book *Giovanni and Lusanna*, on paper it all began on July 14, 1455, when Lusanna's legal representation presented to Antoninus, archbishop of Florence and arbiter of everything nuptial in the city, a suit that maintained that two years earlier Lusanna and Giovanni had been secretly married. According to the documentation and witnesses, Giovanni had brazenly pursued Lusanna for years, following her in the streets and chatting her up in markets and churches, and after her husband died, their acquaintance took a serious turn. Their wedding, as confirmed by multiple witnesses, was presided over by one Fra Felice at the home of Lusanna's brother, Antonio. While some aspects of the union were a bit atypical, like the fact that it was clandestine and didn't involve a dowry or a notary, the secrecy of the wedding was understandable given that Lusanna came from a lower class than did Giovanni. Giovanni's father would disinherit him if he knew he'd married a woman of her social stature, so in theory Lusanna and Giovanni could wed, but they had to keep it under wraps until Papa della Casa died.

Their marriage might have been a secret, but Giovanni and Lusanna's joy was clear as day. According to the case set forth by Lusanna's side, Giovanni spent occasional nights with her, calling out, "Where is my wife?" whenever he entered the house where she remained with her brother. He brought his in-laws pricey gifts like oil and wine and even bought Lusanna a slave girl, Caterina. While the bride continued to wear the dark garb of a widow when out in public, within the safe confines of her brother's home she dressed like any other married woman. More important to the plaintiffs' case, when Lusanna and Giovanni ventured outside the city walls together, to her brother's farm, they openly behaved as a married couple: Lusanna wore a brown tunic that marked her as a married woman, and local peasants saw the couple walking together in the fields, gathering salad greens, exchanging tender greetings. That was the summer of 1454.

But in February 1455, again according to Lusanna's suit, marital bliss went haywire. Giovanni's father died, and rather than publicly declare Lusanna his lawful wife as she expected him to, Giovanni became betrothed to Marietta Rucellai, the fifteen-year-old daughter of one of the most prominent families in Florence. When Lusanna begged Giovanni to nullify the contract he'd made with the Rucellai family, he refused. The moment he became a bigamist, her soul was in mortal danger. Since marriage was a sacrament, her only option was to appeal to the ecclesiastical court.

As you've probably guessed by now, once Giovanni lawyered up, his side of the story was decidedly different: an outright refusal of their marriage. His case rested on the arguments that not only had they never exchanged vows, because a man of his stature would never stoop so low, but Lusanna was, in short, a social-climbing slut. While his team conceded that Giovanni and Lusanna had been lovers for years (twelve years!), the attachment was nothing other than carnal. "Motivated by lust, Lusanna desired to have carnal relations with [Giovanni]," they stated in an affidavit, "for he was young and well endowed . . . and Lusanna was infatuated with him while her husband Andrea was alive and after his death."

First up among Giovanni's many witnesses: Giovanni's upper-class buddies, who could attest to his rank and reputation. They claimed that marriage between someone like Giovanni and someone like Lusanna, no matter how pretty she was, wasn't just unlikely, it was unthinkable.

Second up were Lusanna's former neighbors, including the Magaldis, who she had claimed were witnesses at her wedding. The sordid details of Lusanna's supposed past came tumbling out. Lusanna got around—a lot. Allegedly, she was such a whore that horns (indicating her husband was a cuckold) had been nailed over her doorway! She stared at men hungrily in the street! Lusanna and Giovanni regularly used their neighbors' homes for their rendezvous! There was even the suggestion that she had poisoned Andrea. Claims that would make just about any woman blush flew wildly around the case.

Crucial to this version, however, was the fact that these neighbor witnesses, eighteen in all, were not Giovanni's subordinates just in terms of class but in business as well. Lusanna, her deceased husband, Andrea, and their neighbors were all involved in the cloth industry, and Giovanni was building up his family's mercantile business, which is why he was in the cloth makers' neighborhood in the first place. So close were the relationships between

Giovanni and the artisan cloth makers who were Lusanna's neigh-bors, he was even godfather to some of their children, and it's per-fectly possible some of them owed him money. If ever there was a situation ripe for witness intimidation, this would be it. Giovanni no doubt had the power, the charm, and the money to make his witnesses say what he wanted them to.

Also important was the claim by Giovanni's witnesses that Lusanna made Giovanni repeatedly promise in front of neighbors that he would marry her if Andrea died. If these forced pledges did indeed happen, then they were an indicator of not just her character—so shrewd, so calculating—but also of just how far she might be willing to go in order to get what she wanted, even if it meant murder.

With the advent of what we would now call the cross-examinations, the real mudslinging began. Lusanna's witnesses were called into question because they were of low status, Giovan-ni's counsel even going so far as to allege that Antonio, Lusanna's brother, had been excommunicated from the church for assaulting a priest; Lusanna's representative maintained that Giovanni's wit-nesses (her former neighbors) had conspired to denigrate her, that they were "perjurers, vagabonds, paupers, loiterers in taverns, gam-blers, drunks, pimps, and blasphemers against God."

After two months of rancorous "he said, she said," Archbishop Antoninus and his court decided that someone, somewhere, was clearly perjuring himself—and it *had* to be Giovanni and at least some of his witnesses. Giovanni was ordered to publicly acknowl-edge Lusanna as his lawful wife, treat her with "marital affection" or risk excommunication, nullify his second marriage, and pay a fine of fourteen hundred florins (roughly equivalent to the price of a very nice Mercedes).

It is remarkable that Antoninus, a creature of the elite and the church, ruled in favor of a lower-class woman, but the historian most familiar with the story, Gene Brucker, maintains that Antoninus was a liberal who might have sympathized with her humble roots and knew from experience that the Florentine elite could be ruthless. His written decision indicates that he believed that Lusanna was chaste, but one wonders if he might have privately conceded that it was quite possible that Giovanni and Lusanna had had an affair for years and years but been swayed by the perception that Giovanni was just the type to bribe and frighten witnesses. Perhaps he felt that, in the end, upholding the law and rooting out perjurers was more important than the sordid details of adultery.

Unfortunately, that's not where the story ends. While the details are cloudy, shortly after Antoninus's court's ruling, Giovanni appealed the case before the pope. Six months later word came from Rome that Lusanna and Giovanni's marriage was null and void and that no fine would be levied against Giovanni. Giovanni's tax returns from a few years later list Marietta, his wife, and Caterina, the slave girl whom he had once given to Lusanna, as his dependents.

Gratifyingly, it all didn't come up sunshine and roses for Giovanni. In 1467 he was so in debt, to the tune of four thousand florins to the cardinal of Rouen alone, that he was imprisoned, and in 1478 he was excommunicated, either for defaulting on debt to a cleric or for usury. He died in 1480.

As for Lusanna, she disappears from the historical record after the papal decision annulling her vows to Giovanni. She's not listed in her brother Antonio's household, she's not in the city's tax registers as a widow or a married woman, and she's not in the rosters of people who died within the walls of Florence. She could have been so ruined by the case that her only option was to enter a convent. But it's also possible (and something I hope) that she married a man outside Florence, where maybe once again she was able to gather salad greens with someone she loved.

Heartbreak Behind Holy Walls

When ranking recorded history's most powerful game changers, the microscopic *Yersinia pestis*, the flea-borne cause of the Black Death, just might reign supreme. While historians and microbiologists bicker to this day over how many people died from it (with some figures putting the death toll at 75 to 200 million people over the course of about fifty years, others estimating that 30 to 60 percent of Europe's population succumbed), no one argues with the fact that it turned Europe upside down. The plummet in the number of living persons revolutionized society in a host of ways. Over time it spelled the end of feudalism, because it shifted the balance of power from landowners to agricultural laborers who survived its ravages, which in turn led to the rise of a middle class. It also might have been a contributing factor to the Protestant Reformation, because a dominant theory of the day was that plague was God's way of pointing out that the corrupt and dissolute Catholic clergy had wandered far off course.

In many Italian cities, where up to 80 percent of the population died, countless patrician women ultimately had *Yersinia pestis* to thank for a more stifling kind of change: an arranged marriage to Jesus Christ (and a lifetime of very limited wardrobe choices).

Here's a quick sketch of what happened: It was long the tradition that only one son in a rich family could marry—that way the family's wealth was protected and consolidated. This chosen son would wait until he was in his early thirties to marry, while most upper-class brides were in their late teens. In Europe up until the eighteenth century, a man saying "I do" was synonymous with the most significant influx of assets he'd enjoy in his entire life, while, for a woman, exchanging vows hopefully secured a responsible husband who would properly manage her dowry to safeguard her future.

After the plague struck, however, the population went askew and there simply weren't enough grooms for the brides. Therefore rich families with multiple daughters put all their eggs in one basket, so to speak: They'd make one daughter—their most eligible one (read: the prettiest)—extra attractive with a big fat dowry, while her sisters faced a certain, celibate fate.

Though marriage had always been a bidding process, now the stakes got steadily higher and higher, with dowries ballooning—increasing by almost twofold between about 1400 and 1450. (A pretty, rich bride from Florence, for example, went for about two thousand florins. While assigning currency equivalencies across centuries is dangerous business, sources indicate that around that time two thousand florins might amount to a hefty down payment on a nice house with a two-car garage in the contemporary American Midwest.) Wealthy fathers even set up investment funds to save for their daughters' dowries—the fifteenth-century equivalent of a college fund, just minus the education. Marrying off more than one daughter, much less a physically imperfect one, was simply too expensive a proposition for rich families. Lower-class women also had dowries, albeit far smaller ones. In the middle of the fifteenth century, a servant girl might be worth about fifteen florins (modern equivalent: a few months of groceries for a family of four); a woman with an artisan skill such as weaving might be worth seventy florins (modern equivalent: value of a ten-year-old Honda Civic). Although they were worth less money, lower-class women had far more freedom than did patrician women. They could, for example, go out in public and have some say in whom they married.

This system among the upper class was obviously rife with problems. It was totally against the rules in Italian upper classes for women to marry beneath their social status, *and* it was also unacceptable for them to remain single and at home, so if you weren't the prettiest daughter, you were, putting it frankly, shit out of luck. The solution for the less-than-fortunate daughters? Send 'em to the convents. Jesus would marry just about anyone for a third to one-fifth the going price outside.

It's unclear how many women—a subpopulation one Italian priest (later a saint) memorably termed "the scum and vomit of the world"—were sent off to convents, but surely tens of thousands if not more. It was mass cloistering that resulted in what the historian Silvia Evangelisti describes as a boom in female monasticism. One source indicates that in the mid-seventeenth century in Venice alone, a relatively small city, over two thousand noblewomen were so confined, and in Florence between 1500 and 1799 nearly half of aristocratic females lived out their days behind holy walls, praying eight times a day, never again seeing their natal homes or street life or the glint of sunset on rooftops. In Milan a staggering three-quarters of patrician daughters took the veil. One has to assume most were forced to.

♥ **Book Alert!**

Read more about heartbreak within the walls of an elite Italian convent in Sarah Dunant's absorbing novel *Sacred Hearts*. In it a willful and resourceful sixteen-year-old is forced to become a novice—a nun with probationary status—when her wealthy family discovers that she has fallen in love with her music teacher. She finds an unlikely ally in the convent's apothecary and challenges her fate as yet another star-crossed lover. An accomplished historian, Dunant spins a story that is meticulous in the details and speaks eloquently to the plight of Italy's patrician women in the era of dowry inflation.

The Forty-Year-Old Virgin

The other result from this deluge? While the evidence is at best imperfect, one has to assume there was a lot of rage, depression, grief, and profound sexual frustration within the walls of the better convents.

The last of these is vividly illustrated in the following story—a sort of libidinous *Shawshank Redemption* from Venice's most aristocratic convent. According to Mary Laven's book *Virgins of Venice: Broken Vows and Cloistered Lives in the Renaissance Convent*, in 1614 two nuns, fortysomething Laura Querini and Zaccaria, a younger *conversa* (a servant nun), were discovered to have created a passageway in the convent wall where they had sex with their lovers on numerous occasions. The mere construction of their love nest was no small feat—they'd fashioned a crowbar out of a piece of iron grille wrenched from a cell window, and given that the wall through which they dug was six stones deep, it took them over a month to bust through it. On the outside they camouflaged their work with a large rock and a layer of terra-cotta; on the inside they lined the cavity with lime.

There Laura consummated her relationship with a man twenty years her junior, Zuanne, with whom she'd managed to flirt for years, presumably during visiting hours in the convent parlor. Zuanne brought his cousin to be the *conversa*'s lover. On their first meeting in the hole in the wall—presumably all four of them were packed in there in a scene that brings to mind teenagers on a very advanced double date—the men stayed for several hours, enjoying the pleasures of intercourse with their girlfriends. As if this illicit visit and the literal penetration of the convent walls weren't scandalous enough, it occurred during Lent, the holy weeks before Easter dedicated to abstinence and fasting. After Easter, Zuanne returned alone and stayed in the hole for ten or twelve days nonstop, during which time Laura brought him food and shagged his brains out when everyone else was asleep.

It's unclear exactly how Laura got caught, but she did. Over the course of her subsequent interrogation, Laura recounted how she had first been sent to a convent when she was five or six years old and had taken the veil when she was fifteen. "I took my initial vows at the ceremony of clothing, and later I made my profession," she said. "But I spoke with my mouth and not my heart. I have always been tempted by the devil to break my neck."

Only under threat of torture did Laura reveal the real name of her lover and his cousin, as well as the identities of a servingwoman and a carpenter who had acted as go-betweens. The nuns' lovers skipped town and were sentenced to exile from Venice and the death penalty should they ever show their faces again. For helping get the men to the convent at night, the carpenter was sentenced to eight years of forced labor and assured that should he become physically unable to do his work, he'd be violently relieved of his right hand and tossed in prison. The servingwoman was publicly whipped and promised that if she ever was stupid enough to set foot in a convent again, she would lose her nose and ears.

Just as the historical record is silent regarding how Laura and Zaccaria were caught, so, too, is it about how exactly they were punished by their superiors. But for women who had so single-mindedly pursued activities of the flesh, it's hard to imagine that any punishment would be worse than the life of confinement they'd been sentenced to years and years before. Or maybe, as for Heloise, having experienced and enjoyed sex only to have it taken away forever and ever was its own kind of living hell, and they, too, were tormented by thoughts of intimacy each and every time they prayed.

Escape from Marienthron

The beginning of the end of the forced confinement of women to nunneries and other same-sex institutions is terrifically illustrated in the story of Martin Luther's wife, Katharina von Bora, who was a convent escapee. Luther published his Ninety-five Theses, the cornerstones of the German Protestant movement, in 1517, and somehow, by 1523 or so, Katharina had not only read her future husband's works and been persuaded by them but contacted him to help her escape the convent, Marienthron, where she had lived for years. Luther enlisted the help of a local fish merchant and city councilman by the name of Leonard Köppe to rescue them, and in a scene that can only be described as cinematic, on the night before Easter 1523, Köppe tucked Katharina and eleven other nuns in his wagon, among the fish barrels, and smuggled them out of Marienthron. When they showed up in Wittenberg, Luther's home base nearly 250 miles away, a local observer wrote, "A wagonload of vestal virgins has just come to town, all more eager for marriage than for life. God grant them husbands lest worse befall."[1]

---

1 From Roland H. Bainton's *Here I Stand: A Life of Martin Luther.* New York: Abingdon-Cokesbury Press, 1950: 286–87.

With a little more help from Luther, within two years, all of the women who made it to Wittenberg were married, or at least had homes and jobs—all save Katharina. The plucky young woman had no shortage of suitors, but it seems she'd set her eyes on the prize: She wanted to marry a reformer, preferably Martin Luther himself.

In 1525, Luther married Katharina, and they settled into a marriage that was apparently very happy and filled with good humor. As Luther wrote to an intimate, "There is a lot to get used to in the first year of marriage. One wakes up in the morning and finds a pair of pigtails which were not there before." He referred to her as "my Katie" or "my lord Katie" and depended on her to bring order to his daily life, crowing that "my Katie is in all things so obliging and pleasing to me that I would not exchange my poverty for the riches of Croesus."

When Luther transformed a former monastery into his headquarters, Katie took on the finances, gardening, brewing, and animal husbandry, and ministered to Luther during his many illnesses. Ultimately she presided over a household that included not just their own five children but several orphaned nieces and nephews and four children of a widowed friend, as well as various and sundry servants, boarders, tutors, and refugees. There is of course mighty poetic justice to be found in the fact that a woman who managed to escape a convent (on the eve of the holy day celebrating Jesus's resurrection, no less) wound up modeling for the rest of Europe a new prototype for nuptial unions—the truly loving partnership. While it took the Reformation and the rise of anticlericalism as well as changes in inheritance law another two hundred years or thereabouts to completely dismantle the system that forced so many European women to become nuns, when it finally happened, surely half of the human population breathed a lot easier.

James Achilles Kirkpatrick and Khair un-Nissa, Early-Nineteenth-Century India

In THE DAYS leading up to her sister's wedding in late 1798, Khair un-Nissa, a teenager from an aristocratic Indo-Islamic family, must have dreamed about seeing the man who was the talk of her hometown of Hyderabad. Colonel James Achilles Kirkpatrick was the East India Company's leading representative in the city, and as a favorite of the Mughal royal court he was known for his spectacular diplomatic finesse. Colonel Kirkpatrick was similarly primed to at least see the girl renowned for her sparkling personality and exceptional beauty. But surely neither of them anticipated that they would fall in mad, passionate love and from there build an affectionate and even idyllic marriage, only to have it all collapse, lightning fast.

Love at First Sight

Young Khair un-Nissa's interest in the much older, albeit dashing officer speaks to her beyond-her-years taste for sophisticated men. Colonel Kirkpatrick had a dream job in Hyderabad, one of the richest cities in India thanks to the diamond trade, a post that involved mingling with the local monarch—called the nizam—as well as other high-ranking officials of the Islamic Mughal court, negotiating treaties, and setting up spy networks to keep an eye on the rival French. As detailed in *White Mughals: Love and Betrayal in Eighteenth-Century India* by William Dalrymple, Kirkpatrick was born in India and educated in England, and could effortlessly move between the two cultures, one day playing the Georgian gentleman, complete with games of whist and singing around the piano, the next exercising his fluency in Persian and Hindustani, talking Persian literature with the court poet, and charming the native powers-that-be with his perfect manners. By the time Khair un-Nissa and James first crossed paths, James's passion for all things Indian was his way of life—he smoked hookahs and chewed betel nut, dressed in silk robes and stained his hands with henna patterns, ate his fill of his favorite local dishes, and even went hunting with tame cheetahs. While many of his British colleagues shook their heads in disapproval of the extent to which James had "gone native," doing so clearly made him happy, and no doubt his well-known respect for her culture was, for Khair un-Nissa, part of the attraction.

For much of the 1700s and 1800s, the East India Company dominated large swaths of India, and tens of thousands of British men went there to make their fortunes with the company trading opium, silk, cotton, and tea. For them, keeping *bibis*, or native lovers, was standard operating procedure, and their attitudes toward these women ran the gamut from indifference to adoration. According to William Dalrymple, when asked what he did with his sixteen concubines, one employee of the company said, "Oh, I just give them a little rice and let them run around." Other, more sensitive men included their *bibis* in their wills and were devastated when they lost them. One such gentleman was William Hickey, who fell in love with his very clever and wise *bibi* Jemdandee, who died bearing twins. "Thus did I lose as gentle and affectionately attached a girl as ever a man was blessed with," he wrote.

As for James, his initial interest in Khair un-Nissa was no doubt triggered by her beauty, by her delicacy and her gorgeous eyes, as well as her youth—she was just fourteen years old. Now, before you get on your high horse about how she was a child, it's important to remember that there was nothing wrong with an exchange of glances—probably all that transpired that first encounter—between a man in his late thirties and a teenager in this culture in the 1790s. Moreover, elite women in Hyderabad at this point were often literate and well educated, and in general they led much less restricted lives than did their Middle Eastern counterparts. Sex was far less taboo than elsewhere in the Islamic world, and in harems, called zenanas, dominant wives could wield considerable power. James was no doubt already well accustomed to the allures of aristocratic Mughal women, but while he makes no mention of their meeting in his papers, clearly something special in Khair un-Nissa captured and held his attention.

Upping the Ante

In January 1799, just a month after the wedding where Khair un-Nissa and James Kirkpatrick first saw each other, it was announced that Khair un-Nissa was formally betrothed to a nobleman of her station—a match engineered by her grandfather and one she is reputed to have found "hateful." The moment her grandfather went out of town, Khair un-Nissa's mother, Sharaf un-Nissa, and her grandmother went into overdrive to undermine the engagement. Their best strategy was throwing James and Khair un-Nissa together: They gave her a portrait of him and let him watch her while she slept, she sent him daily messages inquiring after his health when he was sick, and she was even allowed to chat with him from behind a curtain. Then the older women pulled out all the stops by showing up at "the Residency" (the complex where James and other East India Company officials lived) and basically pushing the girl into his bed.

For Khair un-Nissa, facing as she was a marriage to a man who was so objectionable (exactly why is unclear, but it could well have been that the man was violent or had a bad character), sleeping with a man with whom she'd fallen in love at first sight must have seemed like a perfect solution. But for her mother and grandmother, while they likely felt sympathy for her predicament, the advantages to the coupling were probably more political. As Hyderabad's chief British diplomat, James was powerful, and so close was he to the nizam that the latter had honored him with noble Mughal titles such as Mutamin ul-Mulk (Safeguard of the Kingdom), Hushmat Jung (Valiant in Battle), Nawab Fakhr ud-Dowlah Bahadur (Governor, Pride of the State, and Hero). If Khair un-Nissa married him, it would mean a jump in terms of status, power, and assets for her whole family. Looked at from this perspective, Khair un-Nissa was more or less a honeypot, with marching orders not so different from, say, those of the Boleyn girls in the court of Henry VIII.

When rumors of the liaison began to circulate, William Kirkpatrick, James's brother who was living with his own *bibi* elsewhere in India, was alarmed. It was one thing to have an Indian wife or mistress, or even a passel of them, but quite another to have one who was noble and *that close* to the native center of power: Her cousin, Mir Alam, was private secretary to the Mughal prime minister. The concern, of course, was that by literally climbing into bed with a member of Hyderabad's elite, James might compromise his loyalty to Britain.

William pressed James for a confession, and finally, in writing, James admitted to at least some of the details of what he delicately called a "fiery ordeal of a long nocturnal interview with the charming subject of the present letter." In it he confirmed that Khair un-Nissa's mother and grandmother had indeed masterminded the liaison, that she had professed her undying love for him during that first rendezvous under his roof, that he had tried to resist the "tempting feast [he] was manifestly invited to." By James's account it was she who seduced him, and there was nothing dishonorable about it.

What he left out was the fact that his was by no means a short-lived fling, but just the beginning of a very long and hot affair.

Too Close for Comfort

William's concern over his brother's dalliance with a Mughal girl was not unfounded. James and his boss, Richard Wellesley, the overtly racist and greedy governor-general of India, had had a difference of opinion over how to handle the British relationship with the natives (Wellesley was determined to snatch as much as he could from them, while, to James, mutual respect was the name of the game). Their moderately tense professional relationship turned to outrage when Wellesley heard of the affair. James's job was on the line, and some officials even worried that the intimacies of James's private life could trigger a rebellion.

Sure enough, his coziness with the powers-that-be and Khair un-Nissa's family put him in a corner pretty quickly, though probably not in a way that anyone anticipated. When the nizam and the British went to war against the ruler of the kingdom of Mysore, in southern India, in the spring of 1799, the British claimed huge chunks of territory as well as gold plate, arms, armor, silk, and even a solid gold tiger throne—in sum the equivalent of what would now be billions of dollars. When the prime minister, Aristu Jah, accused Mir Alam, his secretary and Khair un-Nissa's cousin, of walking off with the best gems of the spoils, including a necklace of pearls the size of eggs, Mir Alam pressured James to take his side, no doubt thinking that his shared blood with James's lover guaranteed him loyalty. While the ensuing machinations are dizzying, the end result was that in exchange for siding with Aristu Jah over Mir Alam, James received Aristu Jah's protection from terrible rumors that he had raped Khair un-Nissa. In one fell swoop, James became Aristu Jah's poodle and Mir Alam's sworn enemy. Sleeping with Khair un-Nissa had irreversibly complicated his professional relationships.

Yet he continued to see her in secret, and in the summer of 1800, about a year and a half into their affair, Khair un-Nissa got pregnant. A lesser man with a lesser love would have walked away, but not James. He converted to Islam (a move that required circumcision, needless to say an indicator of just how much he was willing to sacrifice for her) and quietly married her. Their son, Mir Ghulam Ali, was born in the spring of 1801, and not long after,

James moved them into the zenana at the Residency. The next year they had a second child, a girl they named Noor un-Nissa.

From Idyll to Darkness

Treaties and concubines were one thing, marriage and conversion to Islam quite another. According to Dalrymple, Wellesley ordered multiple investigations into James's conduct, and James responded by quietly digging his heels in and retreating into his family life, the details of which are charming. When he set about rebuilding the Residency (with financial assistance from the nizam, who by this time had adopted him as a son), he planned elaborate pleasure gardens and fruit orchards (he was particularly proud of his mango trees) and a slide on the rooftop for his children. He also built his children a dollhouse that was a replica of the Residency. From his letters during that period, some details about Khair un-Nissa and the nature of their relationship emerge: She was a devoted, gentle mother and a generous friend, and she was a fan of flying pigeons and designing jewelry and clothing. Together they took on the joint hobby of learning about gems. Thanks to his beautiful home, idyllic family life, dazzling and kind wife, and genuinely affectionate father-son relationship with the nizam, James was the happiest he'd ever been.

But as we all know, perfect happiness can turn on a dime—a cascade of tragedies tipped everything upside down in just a few short years. The nizam died in 1803, followed shortly thereafter by James's friend and protector, the prime minister Aristu Jah. And who should sweep into power but James's enemy, Mir Alam, who had been imprisoned for the four years since the jewel debacle. In that time Mir Alam had become even more hell-bent on revenge, and James was his number-one persona non grata.

And here comes the part that really breaks my heart: When

James and Khair un-Nissa's son and daughter were three and five years old respectively, much as Khair un-Nissa resisted, it was time to ship them off to England to be brought up as proper, well-educated British citizens. Of course the practice of dispatching one's children to an unfamiliar country without their parents seems incredibly cruel and pointless to us now, but then, at least from the British point of view, only an upbringing on English soil could protect Anglo-Indian children from racism. In 1805, Khair un-Nissa said good-bye to her children as they set off with a family friend for Madras, where they were booked on a ship to London. One can only imagine her grief; she knew that it was likely she'd never see them again, and even if she did, after an English upbringing they'd be virtually unrecognizable even to their own mother.

Since he'd booked the children on the ship for England, James had planned on catching up with them in Madras before they set sail, to say their last good-byes. At the last minute, he was called to a meeting in Calcutta, so he revised his plans to go first to Madras, see his children, and then head on to Calcutta. Just before he left, he tried to patch things up with Mir Alam, who stiffly promised by letter, "I will never adopt any measure which may be inconsistent with the relations of friendship or attachment; or incompatible with your wishes." Words of fateful hypocrisy, it turned out.

James's trip on horseback to Madras apparently got off to an auspicious start, but sometime after he crossed the Krishna River, he fell ill. For some time his health had been less than robust due to liver disease. Monsoon rains had made travel difficult, and between the sodden roads and his illness, by the time he reached the port, it was too late—his children had sailed three days earlier. Still sick and surely frantic with grief, he rested for a few weeks and tried to get better, soon pressing on by boat to Calcutta to make his meeting. But when he finally got there, James had to be carried to shore. Then it all went very south very quickly. After adding some codicils to his will, which he'd brought with him knowing that his health could deteriorate quickly, he slipped into a coma. On October 15, 1805, James Achilles Kirkpatrick died at age forty-one, among strangers. He was buried that night, and a piece of equipment he'd ordered that had been waiting for him in Calcutta was immediately auctioned off. As Dalrymple found, one East India Company wife noted in her diary just how cheap life there was: "Here people die one day and are buried the next. Their furniture is sold the third. They are forgotten the fourth."

It took almost three weeks for news of James's death to reach Hyderabad, and there is no record of his nineteen-year-old widow's response. We can only imagine her despair over the fact that everyone she loved most was suddenly gone.

Mourning and Exile

A year after her husband's death, Khair un-Nissa seems to have sufficiently bounced back from the tragedy to make the thousand-mile journey to Calcutta to his grave, accompanied by her mother and Henry Russell, a young, conceited, but talented man who had been her husband's chief secretary. Henry and the two women lived together with their servants all in one house in Calcutta, and there the inevitable happened: Khair un-Nissa, no doubt lonely and bereft, fell into Henry's arms. She was still only twenty, very charismatic, and incredibly vulnerable to the political elite back home. Moreover, according to Muslim tradition then, widows often married the brother of their late husband, and since James's brother William was spoken for and Henry had been loyal to James, Henry was the next-best thing.

As soon as Henry made it clear that he intended to install Khair un-Nissa in a zenana back in the Residency at Hyderabad, shit hit the fan in the highest echelons of power. The British governor-general forbade her to live anywhere except with her own family, but, far worse, just as Henry, Khair un-Nissa, and her mother, Sharaf un-Nissa, made their way back to Hyderabad, word came that Mir Alam—her own cousin—had banished her, on pain of death. Now she had lost not only her beloved family but her home as well.

Before they left India, James arranged for the artist George Chinnery to paint a portrait of his children, and it is just as heartbreaking as everything else about this story. Both children are decked out in Hyderabadi court garb, complete with cascades of pearls, broad sashes, brocade, and slippers with crescent-shaped, upturned toes. Dark-haired, dark-eyed Mir Ghulam Ali meets the viewer's gaze confidently, but the eyes of his sister, Noor un-Nissa, are downcast. She appears puffy-faced from crying. After Khair un-Nissa's death, Henry Russell somehow got his hands on the painting, and by total coincidence, decades later, Noor un-Nissa (who by then was known only as Kitty, since she'd been renamed the moment she got on the ship to England) visited his home in England with a friend, not knowing whose home it was or, one suspects, exactly who its owner was in relation to her mother. Russell avoided meeting her, but he did finally leave the painting to her in his will. For over two hundred years, connoisseurs of British painting in India have recognized it as a master work for its poignancy.

Henry installed Khair un-Nissa in a bungalow in the small, famously smelly town of Masulipatam, and when he hustled back to Hyderabad himself, he discovered that his career there was ruined. Clearly someone with a gift for "moving on," he headed to Madras and promptly fell in love with an Anglo-Portuguese merchant's daughter and married her. So cowardly was he that he dispatched his brother to tell Khair un-Nissa that he'd ditched her to marry someone else. Doubtless Khair un-Nissa was devastated yet again, this time abandoned in a backwater.

In 1809, Mir Alam finally died. Shortly thereafter Khair

un-Nissa returned home, and Henry was made resident, taking up the ambassadorial post James had once held. There is no indication that Henry and Khair un-Nissa saw each other. In September 1813, Khair un-Nissa sent a note to the man who she had once thought was her protector. She was dying. Maybe roused by guilt at long last, Henry invited her to come back to the Residency, where she died within two weeks on the same couch where she had given birth to her daughter eleven years earlier. As the author of *White Mughals* puts it, "There was no clear cause for her condition: she just seems to have finally turned her face to the wall."

She was twenty-seven years old and had known joy with her beloved husband for just five years.

Don't Put Away Your Tissues Just Yet

There is a slightly happy postscript to this terrible tale of woe. Many years later, in 1841, when Katherine "Kitty" Kirkpatrick was nearly forty years old, she received word through Henry Russell that her grandmother back in India, Sharaf un-Nissa, had had her property confiscated and was virtually destitute. From there an amazing correspondence between the two women blossomed, in which both of them unpacked their grief and reconstructed their deep attachment to each other. "I often dream that I see [you and my mother] in the room you used to sit in," Kitty wrote in one letter. "No day of my life has ever passed without my thinking of my dear mother. I can remember the verandah and the place where the tailors worked and a place on the house top where my mother used to let me sit down and slide." Sharaf un-Nissa shared with her granddaughter the story of how her parents met and fell in love. Their tender correspondence lasted six years, until Sharaf un-Nissa died, well into her eighties.

Love in the Time of Communism

IF ONE SPENDS a lot of time thinking about how love and heartbreak play out in history, one inevitably butts up against socialism and communism. When individuals or societies as a whole strive to make the world perfect and equal, what becomes of love relationships, which are inherently imperfect and unequal?

In late-nineteenth- and early-twentieth-century radical political theory, romantic love was often dismissed as a bourgeois trope; the self-centered act of falling in love was the ultimate anticollectivist, antiprogressive quagmire. So how did radicals devoted to the cause of collectivism, which in its most extreme forms demanded renunciation of personal needs, reconcile their political passion with their private lives?

Undoubtedly this chafing between romance and the greater collective good disrupted the love lives of thousands, if not millions, of people, but for our purposes it's worth spending time with one particular couple: Rosa Luxemburg, a Marxist theorist and activist who to this day is a martyr among leftists, and her lover, Leo Jogiches.

Rebel Love

Like so many of the women in this book, Rosa Luxemburg was a shooting star: at once brilliant, brave, unorthodox, and tragic. Even as a teenager, she joined the Proletariat Party in her native Poland (dangerous stuff in the 1880s), and when, aged seventeen, she graduated at the top of her class, she was denied accolades because of her "oppositional attitude toward the authorities." Her career in politics apparently began with organizing a general strike that wound up killing four of her co-conspirators—and at that point she was still in her teens. When threatened with imprisonment in 1889, she fled the underground of Poland for the far more forgiving Switzerland, where she enrolled at Zurich University.

While in Zurich, Rosa became a specialist in *Staatswissenschaft* (political systems), economic and stock-exchange crises, and the Middle Ages; she also fell in mad, passionate love. The object of her affections was another radical, a Lithuanian named Leo Jogiches, four years her senior, with whom she began an affair in 1890, and their fates would be entangled until their untimely deaths. In 1893, when he was just twenty-six and she twenty-two, they founded the Social Democratic Party of the Kingdom of Poland, which agitated for a broad-sweep, international socialist revolution; only if Austria, Germany, and Russia rejected capitalism could Poland be truly free, and an international union of workers was the ticket.

In Rosa and Leo, the industrialized world had one of its first political power couples. They must have made a somewhat odd one at that: She was slight and suffered with an ungainly limp from a childhood hip ailment, but had an exuberant presence, a deadly wit, a beautiful voice, and a compassionate demeanor, while he was known for being a laconic and impatient enigma, albeit a well-heeled one.

While Zurich was a great place to be as a student, at that time the real action was in Germany, where socialist thought was being hashed out in the open. In 1898, Rosa moved by herself to Berlin, even though she worried that doing so would destroy her relationship with her beloved Leo. She quickly became a leader in the Social Democratic Party (SPD), celebrated for her brilliant political theory (she produced hundreds of pamphlets and articles) as well as for her stunning rhetorical skills. She was a political star of the first order; her fans even sent her flowers. But dedicated as she was, the prospect of a normal, modest life always tugged at her. As her biographer Elżbieta Ettinger notes, Rosa wrote one friend years later, when she was even more famous, "I must have *someone* in my life who believes me that it's only by mistake that I circle around the maelstrom of world history, and am really born to tend geese."

With Leo still back in Zurich finishing his dissertation and Rosa based in Berlin but often traveling to speak or do research elsewhere in Europe, they navigated the usual perils of a long-distance relationship and devised a division of labor for their common cause: Rosa was the theoretician and the public face of their ideas, and he was the shadowy mastermind, providing as he did much of the cash to support her activities (he might have been a socialist, but he also had a small fortune in family money at his disposal), editing her work, and issuing instructions. They exchanged hundreds of letters, which provide glimpses of how they jockeyed for dominance in both their personal and professional lives—how they struggled to be both lovers and comrades. He was a cloak-and-dagger kind of guy, and part of him wanted to control her every move, even from hundreds of miles away. "I certainly don't like you telling me not to buy a jacket without you, because I'll buy 'the devil knows what.' . . . If I'm independent enough to perform single-handed[ly] on the political scene, that independence must extend to buying a jacket," she kvetched to him.

The fundamental irony that shows up in her letters is that much as she was the mouthpiece, the flame and the sword of the socialist movement, a huge part of her craved ordinary life with Leo. She called him *dyodyo* (my child) as well as her "husband," and she reminisced about their domestic time together in Switzerland. "We held each other on the road in the darkness and looked at the crescent moon over the mountains . . . carried [groceries] upstairs together . . . the oranges, the cheeses . . . had such magnificent dinners . . . on the little table. . . . I still smell the night's air."[2]

Although his letters to her did not survive, apparently they often lacked intimacy. "Your letters contain *nothing, but nothing* except *The Workers' Cause*," she complained in a letter early on, a gripe that proved to be persistent. "When I open your letters and see six sheets covered with debates about the Polish Socialist Party," she wrote a full decade into their relationship, "and not a single word about . . . ordinary life, I feel faint." Her letters meanwhile were filled with politics and strategy, but also endearing details about her clothing ("I don't walk around like a ragamuffin but look extremely neat [fresh laundered blouses with the black skirt; the summer hat from last year with a veil, still decent looking, will do for every day]"), requests for his input on household goods ("what do you think about buying three decent silver-plated spoons, knives and forks?"), fussing about his diet ("Are you drinking milk? Are you eating eggs?") as well as the requisite ego stroking of her dandyish partner: "My landlady accidently [*sic*] saw [your picture] lying on the table and immediately announced she's ready to divorce her husband for you!"

As time wore on, Rosa wanted all the trappings of a normal domestic life, including a child. In 1900, Leo finally succumbed to

---

2 Letter extracts are from Elżbieta Ettinger's *Comrade and Lover: Rosa Luxemburg's Letters to Leo Jogiches*. Cambridge, MA: The MIT Press (1981).

an ultimatum and moved in with her in Berlin. Their apartment became their home office as things grew still hotter politically. In 1904 she was arrested and imprisoned for insulting Emperor Wilhelm II in one of her speeches, and in 1906 both she and Leo were arrested in Warsaw by czarist police. She was released on bail and returned home; he was sentenced to eight years of hard labor.

Full Collapse

Leo escaped and returned to Berlin, but by then their home was no longer his. Rosa had had it. Both the timing and the details are unclear, but somewhere along the line Leo might have had an affair with a comrade in the underground. By the time Leo got back to Berlin, thirty-five-year-old Rosa was living with the twenty-two-year-old son of a friend, a young man who treated her the way she wanted to be treated.

Things between them were bad for a while—Leo refused to give her up (too little, too late, buddy!), nor would he surrender the keys to the apartment. The scenes between them were dramatic enough that she bought a revolver for self-protection. It might have taken a few years, but over time they settled into a professional relationship that might have been prickly but more or less worked. Her star continued to rise, and in 1913, when she published a book critiquing economic imperialism, called *The Accumulation of Capital*, she was hailed as "the most brilliant head that has yet appeared among the scientific heirs of Marx and Engels."

When war broke out in 1914, however, everything that Rosa had worked toward seemingly shattered. She'd long had a vision of the international proletariat forming a united front, and suddenly socialists from all over Europe had gone nationalist and were favoring what she considered the bourgeois interests of their respective countries. To her, World War I wasn't just "murder on a grand scale; it is also suicide of the working classes of Europe." In response Rosa and her colleague Karl Liebknecht founded a new group that was staunchly antiwar and distributed illegal pamphlets signed "Spartacus"—homage to the gladiator who led a slave revolt against the Romans in the first century BC. For that and surely other infractions, Rosa spent two and a half years between 1915 and 1918—a huge chunk of the war—in prison "for her own protection," only to be released two days before the armistice. From there she and Leo appear to have completely put any rancor behind them and worked tirelessly to promote socialism via the Spartacist League, arguing over and over again that Russia hadn't gotten it right but Germany could.

Immediately after the armistice, Germany erupted in a violent fracas now known as the German Revolution, with the Social Democrats (the party that before the war Rosa had helped lead) duking it out with radicals. In January 1919 the streets of Berlin were a battlefield, and the leader of the Social Democrats ordered the Freikorps—a paramilitary group that was composed of WWI veterans who would become Hitler's storm troopers before long—to put down the radicals once and for all. Rosa and Liebknecht were captured on February 15, 1919, and within hours both were executed. Rosa was first hit in the head with the butt of a rifle and then shot, and her body was dumped in a canal.

Even though Leo and Rosa hadn't been romantic partners for more than ten years, one can only imagine his distress. He was determined to bring her assassins to justice, and while he could have left Berlin in order to save his own skin, he didn't. Within two months he was murdered as well. How fitting it was that both died as martyrs to the cause that had brought them together and kept them together.

· II ·

CULTURE

THERE'S NO WAY of knowing how long human love has graced our planet, but it's fair to imagine that whoever carved the Venus of Willendorf was familiar with the *thump-thump* two hearts can generate in tandem, and literature from a host of ancient cultures (Mesopotamian, Egyptian, Greek, Chinese, Indian) bears plenty of evidence of romantic love.

But while love itself might be universal, how societies filter it and whether it is seen as a good thing or a bad thing, something to be embraced or feared, varies tremendously. The ancient Greeks thought romantic love between a man and a woman was an affliction that called for sorcery to master it, and now, thousands of years later, romantic love is at such a premium we go to great lengths to find and preserve it, whether this means sculpting glowing alter-selves on dating sites and morphing into serial coffee daters to find "the one," passing up marriage proposals in favor of a "Mr. Right" who might not even exist, or breaking the bank on couples counseling when passion fizzles.

As you'll see in this chapter, the way love is *managed* varies widely from culture to culture, whether that means drugging one's husband or injecting tiny furry animals with chemicals and then watching what they do. In the end it's all about the fight to understand love and the struggle with the infinite ways to make it work on both practical and spiritual levels. Love and heart-break are constants, but culture offers infinite ways to wrangle them.

Ancient Greek Love Magic

IMAGINE FOR A moment that you're a fly on the wall twenty-seven hundred years ago on an island off the coast of Italy. A group of Greek men are laughing uproariously over the inscription scratched onto a clay cup from which they're drinking wine: DRINK FROM THIS CUP AND DESIRE FOR A BEAUTIFUL CROWNED APHRODITE WILL SEIZE YOU INSTANTLY is a rough translation. Why so funny? Because that inscription mocks the potions and incantations whipped up by ancient Greek women to make their husbands more affectionate and gentle. For the men gathered around that inscribed cup, drinking from it might have been a little like a frat-boy idea of a good joke.

In 1958, archaeologists excavating the ruins of Pithekoussai—one of the early ancient Greek colonies dating from the beginning of classical antiquity—unearthed this cup. The inscription is one of the earliest known examples of Greek text, and it's also early evidence of the fabulously gendered ancient Greek practice of love magic.

Philia: *The Secret to a Happy Marriage*

According to the classicist Christopher A. Faraone, author of *Ancient Greek Love Magic*, ancient Greek classical texts are rife with allusions to love magic: Charmed golden apples slung like bowling balls aided in the seduction of Atalanta, the Sirens lured sailors with their songs, and naturalists and medical writers meticulously recorded how plants and animal parts could be deployed to loverly advantage.

Historical records indicate that women in ancient Greek culture typically turned to magic when their husbands were being grouchy, inattentive, or just plain unaffectionate. Through charms, ointments, or potions, women pursued domestic harmony, or what classicists refer to as *philia*—a nonthreatening form of affection and love, which might include sex. But what these women thought of as a little harmless sorcery would actually be considered *poison* from our modern perspective.

> When the women of ancient Greece appealed to a deity for help with love problems, they typically turned to Aphrodite, the goddess most associated with love, also known for having entered the world as a naked adult and for taking lovers in spite of the fact that she was married. By invoking Aphrodite when they cast a spell, women were asking for her guidance in maximizing the efficacy of their concoctions and incantations—as if each of them were Aphrodite's apprentice.

First the sex stimulants: While wine was often the first prescription for an inattentive husband, the next stop was likely crushed blister beetles, *Lytta vesicatoria*, which we now know contains cantharidin—an odorless, colorless compound that in tiny amounts causes erection in males. Today crushed blister beetles are better known as the illegal substance "Spanish fly," but back then the irritant was readily available and dosages were approximate. Ancient Greek literature is peppered with hand-wringing over well-meaning wives who went a little heavy on the beetle seasoning. A woman in quest of a stiffer husband could well wind up with a regular ol' stiff instead.

But while smashed bugs might make a man more amorous, it seems that many ancient Greek wives were less interested in exciting their husbands than they were in soothing them. And for that, according to Faraone, they turned to narcotics. Among the ingredients used in *philia* concoctions were mandrake, root of cyclamen, and oleander—all of which are mildly narcotic in small doses and downright lethal in large ones. And most of the allusions in ancient Greek texts to the use of *philia* magic are in reference to big shots. It would be as if all the G8 leaders' wives drugged their respective husbands in order to make their homes, the immediate neighborhood, and the world a nicer place—even if it meant that they might kill them in the process.

♥ Modern Love Spells

Knowing what we know now about toxins, barring a nice glass of cabernet, most ancient Greek *philia* potions are these days out of the question. Should you want to dabble in love spells, however, there's no shortage of them to be had online, typically on sites featuring lots of pentagrams. Often these spells require candles (preferably pink) and rose petals or oil, and occasionally crystals or apples. One memorable spell I came across can be deployed when your loved one is not treating you right, and it involves carving an apple open like a jack-o'-lantern and inserting a slip of paper bearing his name and birth date, along with a photo of him and three spoons each of honey and sugar (preferably brown and organic). Then you should put the top of the apple back on, wrap it up in your underwear, place the parcel in a container, and stick it in the back of your closet until it gets mushy. Once said apple is mushy enough (and has presumably saturated your underwear), remove it from the container and bury it.

Arugula, Apples, and Agōgē—Quickly, Quickly!

While ancient Greek women relied on drugs to get a well-behaved, docile husband, their male counterparts relied on salad, drugs, fruit, and what we might now call violent mumbo jumbo in order to get a little *eros*—otherwise known as, shall we say, action of a sexual nature.

Men often used potency spells on themselves, a sort of ancient Greek equivalent of Viagra. A man might, for example, use a cream to increase the duration of an erection. (Faraone describes how one fourth-century-BC drug was rumored to produce twelve erections in succession. Three maybe, but *twelve*?) Others would eat arugula, which was supposed to induce ardor, or wear an animal part associated with potency. (Apparently the right testicle of a donkey could be fashioned into a woody-inducing bracelet.) Many of the ingredients used to stimulate male animals kept for breeding, like stallions, doubled as human-male stimulants. Advice was blunt: "To copulate a lot, bruise the seed of arugula and small pinecones and drink on an empty stomach" and "To screw a lot, drink, in advance, celery and arugula seed." These prescriptives were no different from, say, Prolongze, ExtenZe, Zenerx, Vigrex, and other male-enhancement drugs oft advertised in the back pages of *Sports Illustrated* or *Cigar Aficionado*.

A man with good aim could also rely on an apple or other seeded fruit to get what he wanted, as inferred from repeated references in texts of the era to a man taking a bite from an apple and then tossing it into the lap of a woman he wished to seduce. If she liked him, she'd tuck it into her girdle, hence the Hellenistic epigram that translates as "I hit you with an apple. And you, if you willingly love me, receive it and give me a share of your virginity." The modern equivalent to this apple tossing might be, say, "Your place or mine?" or "Want to come up for a drink?" Acceptance of the apple, like acceptance of the invitation to come up and see the etchings, indicated consent.

But far kinkier (and more removed from our own practices) were *agōgē* spells—literally "carrying away" or "abduction"— which at their most powerful were effigy and incantation combos that men turned to in order to make women hop into the sack.

Thanks in part to the survival of a cache of handbooks belonging to a magician who lived and worked in Egypt in the late fourth or early fifth century BC, we know the basic formula for a typical *agōgē* spell: one effigy of a woman (typically kneeling, with her feet and hands bound); a baker's dozen of pins or needles; burning of said effigy; requests that the woman be so distracted by thoughts about her admirer that she can't sleep, eat, or drink; demands that the woman leave her family and climb into his bed; and the closing phrase "Quickly, quickly, quickly!"

A smitten man might stop off at his local magician's to purchase an effigy of a woman and a spell prepared by a scribe. Back in the privacy of his own home, he'd pierce the effigy with thirteen pins—one for every orifice, one for each hand and foot, and one right over the heart.

He might then burn the effigy over an open fire stoked with myrrh and chant something to the effect of:

> Make this woman sleepless, night after night, because she thinks only of me. Deny her food and water. Yank her from her friends and family by her hair and her intestines until she is with me. Make her burn with desire for me, force her to come have sex with me. Enter her through her *psuche*[3] and live

---

3 A puzzling term that apparently could simultaneously mean "soul" and operate as slang for female genitalia.

in her heart and marrow until she comes to me and brings me her everything. If she is tempted by another man, make her push him away and come to me! Quickly, quickly, quickly!

Then, just to further prove exactly how devoted he was, our young hero might seal the little lady in a clay pot with a tablet on which the spell had been inscribed and bury her.

Should this scenario not be sufficiently . . . ahem, alternative for you, let's not forget that the torture of a small animal could make an *agōgē* spell truly unstoppable. For example, as Faraone describes, one might dump hot coals on a live lizard; fasten a small, "lascivious"[4] bird to a wheel and whip and burn it (so that its "madness" would transfer to the object of the man's affection); pluck out the eyeballs of a live bat, deposit them in the eye sockets of a clay dog, and pierce the dog with pins; maim chameleons; or torture a puppy to death. While these options might have been enough to make Jeffrey Dahmer blush, more sensitive suitors had the option of painting an erotic spell on the wings of a live bat that would then be released—the bat's nocturnal ways, coupled with the spell, would ensure that the victim was rendered sleepless.

Agōgē spells performed by women on men were apparently very few and far between. But one of the few extant ones is telling, because it combines the violence of a man's *agōgē* spell with the desired outcome of a *philia* spell: "Melt away his heart and suck out his blood in his love, in his passion, in his pain . . . until he comes to me and performs all my wishes and continues loving me, until he goes off to Hades." (We can only assume that "performs all my wishes" = take the garbage out, stop performing *agōgē* spells, and for the love of Zeus, stop ogling the slave girl's ass.)

---

4 A "lascivious" bird was apparently one that moved its neck or tail in a particularly lustful manner.

Magic Schmagic

At face value I love that women practiced "magic" that wasn't magic at all—it was pharmaceutically sound, if dangerous—while men practiced "magic" that was, science tells us, patently ridiculous. But it is important to try to understand these rituals within their own cultural context. In *Ancient Greek Love Magic*, Faraone explains that *eros*—the raison d'être of *agōgē* spells—was "defined as dangerous, unwelcome, and irresistible lust." It was all about getting laid—the quick fix to an unwanted affliction. (Little did the Greeks know that orgasm actually increases attachment rather than decimates it.) Erotic love was, to the ancient Greeks, more on a par with epilepsy or stroke than warm fuzzies. So within the context of a culture that was very suspicious of erotic love, *agōgē* spells had more in common with curses—like the type one would use against a sworn enemy—than they did with their more gentle, feminine counterpart, *philia*-inducing concoctions. *Philia* practices, on the other hand, are best understood as healing rituals.

We live in a society that embraces therapy, so it's hard to not look for the psychological or therapeutic subtext of *agōgē* practices. Did a lovesick man who cast an *agōgē* spell subconsciously identify with the effigy or was it a plea for catharsis? Did projecting his pain onto a miniature woman help to alleviate his pain? Did the spell itself inspire self-confidence, so the next time he saw the woman in question, he'd pitch a real or proverbial apple a little closer to home plate?

Faraone's interpretation of *agōgē* rituals posits that while these appear to be violent sex spells, they might really have been about marriage in a society where social advancement relied on marrying up. In other words, these men weren't smitten or lovesick—they were merely being pragmatic. A man would cast a spell on a woman he wanted to marry to ensure that she would break her emotional ties with her natal family and "bring everything she has" to him—a hefty dowry. Symbolic violence and a figurative kidnapping were viewed as necessary to make her trade her loyalty to her father for loyalty to her husband.

> If *agōgē* did exaggerate or fake men's violent impulses toward women, then they might have been similar to a particular form of bride kidnapping among the ancient Greeks, in which a groom snatched a bride away from her home, but with her own and sometimes her parents' private consent. This kind of staged bride kidnapping could cover for a love marriage or an unplanned pregnancy or save face for everyone if a bride's dowry was insufficient. The modern honeymoon, by the way, could well be a relic of ancient bride kidnapping, when a groom hid his bride from her family for at least a month after snatching her to ensure that there was time to get her pregnant.

Over time women began to appropriate *agōgē* magic, and, according to Faraone, by the classical period courtesans and prostitutes in particular turned to traditionally male spells to increase their customer base. So, for women, not only did its applications expand to nondomestic situations but they became another tool in an ambitious businesswoman's arsenal. Ultimately, when practiced by women, both *philia* and *agōgē* must have been about exercising power in a society that was incredibly male-dominated. Drugs and spells might well have been the only way, or at least the easiest way, for women to feel some level of empowerment.

Heartbreak: The Metaphor

Butterfingers, rule of thumb, iron fist, brain fart, sweet tooth, brownnose, lip service, camel toe, pain in the ass, shot in the arm, egghead, brain freeze, elbow grease—these are just a few of the more colorful bodily metaphors that spice up the English language.

♥ A Sampling of Heart Metaphors

Bleeding heart, heart of gold, sweetheart, take heart, heart-to-heart, wear your heart on your sleeve, learning by heart, change of heart.

Metaphors aren't just decorative bits of trim that dress up an otherwise ordinary exchange of thoughts. In the past thirty years or so, cognitive linguists have come to believe that metaphors exist to ease our understanding of abstract ideas by making comparisons in words. "Life," for example, becomes more comprehensible if it is compared to a "journey." And metaphors, we now know, cross domains: They are fundamental not just to language but also to thought, culture, body, and, significantly, the workings of the human brain. Metaphors actually shape the way we think.

At first glance "heartbreak" would appear to fit right in with terms such as "brownnose" and "elbow grease," since it, too, relies on a body part, but it is in fact quite different in the eyes of cognitive linguists. "Heartbreak" is what linguists refer to as a "primary metaphor," because it is rooted in a bodily sensation that is connected to an emotional state. Just about everyone *feels* heartbreak, but no one *feels* a brainstorm or elbow room. (And let's not even go there with what the physical sensation of a brain fart might be, much less how it would affect pillow talk.)

When a bodily experience is universal, so is the metaphor. If one were to literally translate "camel toe," for example, into any other language and ask what it meant as metaphor, a native speaker would likely give you a puzzled stare, but render "heart" and "break" into any other language and he'll know exactly what you're talking about. Chances are good that his own language is studded with a similar term that is some combination of "heart" and "break."

♥ "Heartbreak" in Other Languages

összetöri valaki szívét (uhsuh-tuhree valakee seevayt) = break someone's heart (Hungarian)

разбитое сердце (razbitoye serdtse) = "shattered" + "heart" (Russian)

心碎 (xin sui) = "heart" + "shatter" (Chinese)

un coeur brisé = "broken heart" (French)

el corazón roto = "broken heart" (Spanish)

crepacuore = "sudden death" + "heart" (Italian)

미|苦 (bitong) = "sadness" + "pain" (Korean)

patah hati = "broken liver" (Indonesian)

In fact, many emotions are constructed similarly across languages: Fear is often cold ("cold feet"), happiness is often up ("floating on cloud nine"), anger is often hot (or more specifically, a hot liquid or gas in a container, as in "boiling with rage"), and affection is warmth ("warm friendship"). Emotions are also often rendered as forces in metaphors—hence the "break" in "heartbreak."

A notable variation in the universal "heart" + "break" idea is *patah hati* ("broken liver") in Indonesian. Indonesian culture assigns the seat of the emotions to the liver rather than the heart, thanks to an ancient divination ritual in which the livers of sacrificed animals were examined for messages from the gods about humans' fates or characters. In Indonesia the liver is associated with love in just the same way the heart is in most other languages and cultures; consider the charming example *buah hati*, which means "fruit of the liver," a metaphor for children conceived in a love relationship. But don't think that the association between the liver and love is unique to Indonesians; among ancient Babylonians, Assyrians, Etruscans, Hebrews, and Greeks, the liver was also associated with love and emotion. And it's probably no accident that in German the word for love (*Liebe*) so closely resembles the word for the internal organ (*Leber*).

It's even possible that metaphors help determine the behavior they represent. As one specialist in metaphor, Zoltán Kövecses, wrote, "Our metaphors of emotion can be considered, to an extent, as veiled instructions on how to behave when emotional."[5]

Just ten little letters: H-E-A-R-T-B-R-E-A-K. But is the word the master of the body or is the body the creator of the word?

---

5 From Zoltán Kövecses's *Emotion Concepts*. New York: Springer Verlag (1990).

Matchmaking:
The Second-Oldest Profession

Much as it might offend our Western sensibilities, match-making and arranged marriages are still de rigueur in many cultures, although how it's done, as well as why, varies widely. Among traditional Turks a young man might signal his readiness to get married by a deliberate show of grumpiness, in which case his mother puts the wheels in motion to find him a suitable wife while his father stands aside, maintaining the requisite emotional distance that society expects between fathers and sons. In Kenya the Meru, a Bantu tribe, rely on what we'd think of as a maddeningly obtuse metaphorical exchange in order to determine whether a match can be made: The boy's father might ask the girl's father if there was any water nearby to be had, and if his daughter was already engaged, the girl's father would say that someone had already drunk the water. But if his daughter was available and it seemed like a good match, they'd strike a deal and skip the water to instead share a ceremonial beer.

For many societies, marrying up is the name of the game, but in Egypt, according to ethnographers, it's not considered to one's advantage to marry above one's station—doing so is asking for trouble, because then one partner is inevitably more sophisticated than the other and will have too-high expectations. And then among some Jewish communities, there is a very practical and scientific justification that organizations exist for matchmaking: With DNA analysis, they're able to weed out incompatible genetic matches that can result in Tay-Sachs disease, cystic fibrosis, and Canavan disease in a couple's progeny. Sure, matchmaking is just plain practical in many traditional societies, but it can also head off all manner of heartbreaks, and not just romantic ones.

Let's take a close look at the rise, fall, and present state of matchmaking and arranged marriages in China, India, and yes, even here at home.

Never Match an Ox with a Dog

In China before the twentieth century, marriages were almost always arranged, and the basic foundation for it was *men dang hu di*—the idea that both families should be of the same social and economic status. Typically, when a child became an adolescent, the parents enlisted the help of a professional matchmaker (usually an elderly married woman with excellent people skills) who was armed with the basics about every eligible person in her community. She made it her business to constantly propose matches until she hit the sweet spot.

As detailed in the book *Mate Selection Across Cultures*, while matchmakers proposed an initial match based on *men dang hu di*, when it got down to the families making an actual decision, they pulled out Chinese superstition's big guns: ancestors and zodiac signs. Once a family approved a boy as a possible mate for their daughter, the matchmaker would write down the time and date of the girl's birth on a piece of paper, take it to the boy's family, and there it would sit on their ancestral altar for three days. If after three days nothing bad happened ("bad" being anything from a stomachache to a death in the family), then both sets of parents would move on to the next step—consulting an astrologer to see if their children's zodiac signs were compatible. Now, if *that* proved to be a bad match (never set up an ox with a dog or a rat with a rabbit), then the deal was immediately called off. If, however, the zodiac signs proved compatible, then the boy's family would give the girl's family a slip of paper with *his* birth details, they'd set it on their altar for three days, and provided that no indigestion or dislocated shoulders descended on the family . . . well, then they were good to go.

To many of us, this system seems curious, but given that China was traditionally a collectivist society, it made perfect sense. Moreover, in a culture where elders and ancestors were revered, it was logical that important decisions like whom to marry weren't left to the inexperienced young. And while it's certainly impossible to ascertain just how many good marriages came out of this system, we can't discount the fact that an arranged marriage could be a very caring, even passionate one, while, as we all know, a love match can easily deteriorate into bitterness and profound disappointment. As one elderly Chinese man who had an arranged marriage in 1940 put it, because he "dated" his wife only *after* marrying her, their union was "cold at the start but hot at the end."

While arranged marriages were outlawed the year after the communists came to power in 1949, over time love, rather than political stature or job prestige in the communist order, became a solid prerequisite for a successful marriage, and these days dating and premarital sex, particularly in the "love haven" of college, are very much the norm.

Traditional Chinese culture boasted a particularly nifty variation on arranged unions called a "ghost marriage," in which a living person, usually a woman, married a dead man. A ghost marriage could be deployed if a bride's fiancé died, so she could still have the protection of his family. But in the early twentieth century, ghost marriages became popular among women resistant to marriage, particularly those who were silk producers in the Canton Delta and wanted to be financially independent. According to historians, competition for a dead man's hand was fierce, with women reporting that "it's not so easy to find an unmarried dead man to marry."

Good Dharma

Now let's look at India, where globalization and modernization have taken firm root, where women are commonly elected to the highest government positions, and where around 95 percent of Hindu marriages are arranged.

Just as in traditional China, Indian culture champions collectivism—the greater good and the family's success over individuals' happiness. And also as with China, elders are expected to have the best judgment when it comes to a mate for a young person, with young people often agreeing that their parents have known them their whole lives and have their best interests at heart. Their best interests, moreover, are rooted in compatibility over the long term rather than romantic love at the outset. Even among educated upper-middle-class women who could choose to find a mate themselves, arranged matches are often preferred for a host of reasons, not the least of which is surely that an arranged marriage qualifies as *dharma* (righteous), while a marriage not arranged by one's kin is seen as *adharma* (nonrighteous). Overall, women in *dharma* marriages are better respected than their *adharma* counterparts. Finally, there is more collective accountability in an arranged marriage. If the going gets rough, the parents involved are more likely to play a supportive role, guiding the couple toward peace and productivity, whereas in a love marriage when things go south, a couple is on their own when it comes to sorting things out.

The matchmaking process often goes something like this: A young person's elders (parents, aunts and uncles) pay a visit to a broker who will have listings of hundreds or even thousands of candidates, or maybe they'll post an advertisement online or in the newspaper. What they're looking for is someone who is a good match in terms of education, class, and family values. Once the pool is narrowed down to the most promising candidate and both families agree to meet, they might all gather at someone else's home, a country club, or a restaurant. The prospective couple might chat alone or go off to a local coffee shop while the parents size up one another. Everyone is keenly aware that this is a pairing of two families as much as it is of two people, if not more so.

If everyone is game, the next step is to exchange horoscopes, with the prospective couple's compatibility rated by factors like their behaviors and interests, their attraction to each other, their "nature match" (e.g., never put two people with hot tempers together), emotional sturdiness during crises, and longevity of life. All of the factors add up to thirty-six points or *gunas*. If one's prospective mate gets a score of less than eighteen *gunas*, then the deal is off. Eighteen to twenty-four *gunas* is thought to result in an average match, twenty-five to thirty-two *gunas* counts as a very good match, and if the score is more than thirty-two points, then you've got yourself a winner. (And if for any reason one or the other party wants out, then either family can fall back on the horoscopes and say it just wasn't a good match according to the stars, and everyone saves face.)

Then, after a quick negotiation over things like who is going to pay for the wedding, what sort of gifts the bride's family will throw in to sweeten the deal (which could be cash, furniture, gold jewelry, land, or pots and pans, but these are not contractual obligations), they get married. Long engagements are sometimes frowned upon as risky, and sometimes it's a matter of days from first meeting to wedding night. A couple can use the time between the engagement and the wedding to date and become romantic.

Now, many Westerners are quick to vilify arranged marriages like these. They're seen not only as completely lacking in romance but demeaning to women, a terrifying example of the mad clutch of patriarchy. Moreover, there are plenty of ways an arranged marriage can be less than perfect, not the least of which is that Indian brides leave their natal homes to live with their husband and often their husband's parents. For many a bride, issues arise not so much with her husband as with her mother-in-law—the real keeper of power in domestic life.

But as increasing numbers of Indian women are becoming better educated and seek careers outside the home, we have to ask the question, why has arranged marriage endured? The answer just might be "Because it works." Of course not every arranged marriage is happy, but plenty are, and plenty of *dharma* couples recount their very first meeting with a narrative that sounds an awful lot like love at first sight. Maybe arranged marriage is far more empowering to a woman than an outsider might think. Falling in love, after all, means loss of power. Marriage is a long, difficult haul, and romantic love too often has a short life span and ends unhappily. Maybe the enduring nature of arranged marriage in India, a country that otherwise has rocketed toward modernity, is due to an update of the tradition. It's as if the culture kept the good things about arranged marriage—the careful selection of an appropriate mate, guided by loved ones—and dumped many of the bad parts, like the emphasis on property (dowries, or the contractual property exchange involved in marriage, were officially outlawed in 1961). Well-crafted arranged marriages might result in *less* heartbreak and result in fewer fractured (and fractious!) marriages, thereby underpinning a more stable society. The divorce rate in India is 1.1 percent, while in the United States it is, staggeringly, 50 percent. Maybe that's a trade-off worth thinking about.

I Have a Friend Who Would Be Perfect for You!

For all the demonizing we may do of cultures' matchmaking ways, we sure do love to dabble in it ourselves, whether it's watching the ridiculous shenanigans of *The Millionaire Matchmaker* on TV or setting up a friend with the cute guy four cubicles over.

Rules for the Matchmaker

1. Blind dates, in which both parties know they're being set up, are a risk. A more graceful and strategic way to bring two people together is to invite them both to the same event and introduce them but only give one the heads-up. This way, natural chemistry can take its course with less pressure, and if the person who is in the know decides he or she is not interested, then no harm done.
2. Never set up two people just because they're both single. That's just plain offensive. Before you embark on the setup, take the time to write down why you think the couple might be a good match.
3. Keep your distance from the results.

Rules for the Matchmade

1. Much as it might be tempting to get drunk on a blind date or setup, please don't.
2. Even if you really, really dig the person you're set up with, resist sleeping with him or her the first night. A setup is a strangely sacred thing; respect it, and the person who set you up, with your best behavior. Save the hanky-panky for the second date!
3. If it doesn't work out, don't draw your matchmaker into it. Keep your mouth shut and move on.

It strikes me that the perils of playing matchmaker to our friends and acquaintances are many. Sure, there's always the slim chance that a fix-up will actually spawn a successful and enduring relationship, yet it's far more likely that one person will dig the other but the feelings aren't mutual, or that they can't stand each other, or that they fall in love at first and then split up and blame you or want you to take sides, or, worst of all, that one person is so disgusted by the other that he or she takes personal offense that you set them up at all.

Given all the possibilities for a fix-up to fall flat, something pretty powerful drives the determined matchmaker, and I think in some ways that drive is at its core both primal and vainglorious. We live in a fractured society, and perhaps this explains why some of us are so invested in the setup—it speaks to an innate need to make connections, to feel a part of something. If the match takes, all the better—the matchmaker can claim the credit for creating something out of nothing. Ultimately, however, I think there's a bit of religion in our culture's matchmaking: Playing Cupid is the closest we'll ever come to being God.

Debunking Monogamy

Scientists are increasingly coming around to the notion that some mammals grieve over the loss of loved ones. Elephants are downright reverent when presented with the bones of their deceased brethren, dolphin mothers appear to grieve when their calves die, dogs and cats sometimes express what sounds an awful lot like grief when a close animal friend dies. But, importantly, these are not examples of mated pairs. There is in fact no documented case in the animal world of both partners in a mated pair dying in quick succession, with the second dying of heartbreak over the loss of the first. Among humans, sure (the term for it is "broken heart syndrome"—the phenomenon when one spouse dies shortly after the other, like Johnny Cash passing away just four months after his beloved wife, June), but among the furred and feathered who mate, death by heartbreak is a big fat myth. When one half of a mated pair dies, the other doesn't also curl up and die. It moves on and finds a new mate.

Yet if I had a nickel for every time someone suggested I include a chapter on animals who die when their mate dies . . . well, I wouldn't be rich, but I'd sure have enough change to buy a new pair of socks. This, I think, is because in our culture we cling to, or even manufacture, any evidence that can prove that monogamy—mating for life, exclusively and without question—is natural.

No matter what you call going outside a primary relationship for sex—infidelity, breach of monogamy, or regular ol' cheating—one study by the Market Facts research firm indicated that it's the number-one reason women cite when asked about the cause of their most recent breakup, while men rank "we grew apart" at the top. If that's the case in your particular situation, and you firmly believe that sexual monogamy is what does and should distinguish humans from their amoral, less discriminating furry and feathered relations, then you might not want to read further.

Or maybe you do.

Flirtatious Fauna

Swans. Lovebirds. Blackbirds. Birds have long been the animal kingdom's faces of fidelity, to the point where 90 percent of the ten thousand or so species known were thought to be strictly monogamous—whether for just one breeding season, like penguins, or even forever, like geese. But DNA analysis in recent studies has debunked this persistent myth, showing that 40 percent of nestlings are tended to by a father figure who is *not* their biological father (a finding that can't help but lead one to imagine Maury Povich shouting to a goose or pigeon, "YOU ARE NOT THE FATHER!").

Among the roughly four thousand mammals in the animal kingdom, the percentage of monogamous species is lower than that in birds (about 3 percent). Gibbons, beavers, otters, a few foxes, and prairie voles have traditionally gotten a pat on the head for monogamy, and, like birds, many are masters of the long-term relationship. But, scientists are finding out, it appears that there's a big, big difference between monogamy as in "never have sex with anyone else" and what's called "social monogamy"—raising a family together but indulging in an occasional fling.

From an evolutionary point of view, what animal behaviorists call "extra-pair copulations" among animals that live as mated pairs but are sexually unfaithful makes sense. The males benefit by increasing the odds that their genetic material will be passed on via multiple females, while the females benefit from the truism that we human women scrape against repeatedly in our love lives: The best-looking sperm donor and the most reliable provider don't always come in the same package.

For those who believe in strict, ever-faithful monogamy, this can be a hard pill to swallow. We wish very badly for a sign—a scientific sign!—that having only one sexual partner is natural. But maybe it's not, and maybe we owe this little misunderstanding (or willful ignorance, depending on how you look at it) to the rise of the love marriage.

What's Love Got to Do with It?

For most of human history, "mated pairs" among humans—aka "marriage"—have been about three overlapping things: property, politics, and labor. For both elites and common people around the globe, marriage meant a transfer of property, usually through a dowry. Dowries could mean instant gain in tangible assets ("If you marry my daughter, I'll throw in an extra five cows") and, in some cases, added political power ("Marry my daughter and I'll give you a third of France, plus I'll send soldiers if anyone attacks you"). And, as mentioned earlier, for the laboring classes, saying "I do" was about finding a good workmate. If you were a farmer, then you wanted a mate who could plow fields; if you were a weaver, a woman who was adept at spinning would be a good choice. Bluntly stated, between one's need for a labor partner, limited choices, and a generally dreary hardscrabble existence, romantic love wasn't a priority.

Divorce might be in some measure a cultural adaptation. In previous eras high mortality rates meant that men and women often lost their spouses and remarried, thereby justifying what is probably the natural impulse toward serial monogamy. But as people became healthier and lived longer, pairings lasted longer; divorce might well have become more common in part because it's another way to fulfill a natural need for variety.

So what do you have, then, with a marriage that is rooted in practical matters rather than in passionate, romantic love? By our standards, lots more tolerance for extra-pair copulations, particularly for men.

♥ The Na on Marriage: Nada!

According to historian Stephanie Coontz, the only society known not to have anything resembling marriage is one in southwestern China, called the Na. Babies are made during discreet liaisons at night, often via casual relationships. Sexual partners are under no financial obligations to each other, and children are raised jointly by brothers and sisters who live together and are one another's lifelong companions. Some sibling-based Na households go back ten generations.

In one study of 109 societies, only 48 forbade extramarital sex to both husbands and wives—fewer than half, even *after* globalization has made the modern, Western model of love marriage the ideal. And both now and historically, countless cultures have not regarded monogamous sexual fidelity as the primary ingredient for a successful marriage. Many have even regarded extramarital sex as completely normal. According to historian Stephanie Coontz, in ancient China it wasn't unusual for women to have their sisters join them as "backup wives"; in the regions around Nepal, Tibet, and northern India, a woman might be married to brothers, all of whom get to sleep with her (though presumably not all at once); and Eskimos long had "co-spousal" or "reciprocal spousal-exchange" relationships in which two couples would swap partners, jealousy was regarded as "boorish," and the two couples' children were all regarded as siblings. And our gendered assumption that what's traditionally been okay for the gander has not been okay for the goose doesn't always hold. There are plenty of cultures that allow a woman to have sex with a man other than her husband—it's a practice called "wife loaning," even though the term implies, incorrectly, that it's not the woman's idea. As soon as she's married, for example, a Dogon woman (West Africa) can openly pursue an extramarital tumble in the millet with her mother's blessings (a notion that would cause *my* mother, who taught me at a young age that "boys don't like used goods," to go into cardiac arrest).

Bonus, Not Rule

None of this is to say that in earlier eras married people never loved each other—surely many did. But as Coontz puts it, "love in marriage was seen as a bonus, not as a necessity." Then along with the Enlightenment in eighteenth-century Europe came the notion that one had the right to free choice and to happiness. Ergo, one had the right to marry for love. And with that came the notion that the ideal marriage should be emotionally intimate and, above all else, sexually exclusive. Sure, marriages rooted in property and politics still continued, and people still fooled around on the side, and as recently as the nineteenth century good husbands could still enjoy their little peccadilloes and wives would look the other way. Even among the Victorians, a pesky case of the clap contracted from a prostitute didn't mean that a marriage was over. Particularly among the upper classes, married men could have mistresses and visit courtesans with impunity, and while married women in European culture have never had quite equal freedom in that department, there are settings in which the rules can be relaxed. In upper-class British society, for instance, if a married woman had already produced heirs fathered by her husband, she could engage in affairs, as long as she was discreet and didn't get pregnant. Even Princess Diana operated behind this shield, having multiple affairs after William and Harry were born but before she and Prince Charles divorced.

Slowly but surely, though, love and sex—which even science now tells us are often irrational and inconstant, complex and nonexclusive—became the requirement for a successful marriage. It might have taken a few centuries, but over time we arrived at the notion underpinning society's most enduring institution now: that any sexual act outside it spells THE END.

The Savage Maybe?

In 2011 the *New York Times Magazine* published an article called "Married, with Infidelities," that was part essay on marriage and monogamy, part profile of the sex columnist Dan Savage, who is gay and in a socially but not sexually monogamous relationship (he calls it "monogamish"). Savage pushes his readers to think hard about how the expectation of monogamy has affected modern marriage. And while the profile was written by a man, Mark

Oppenheimer, who made it clear that he himself is married, monogamous, and faithful to his wife, he clearly thinks that Savage has a point: Maybe monogamy, as in if you're in an LTR and you never sleep with someone else, is not realistic for every individual or every relationship. No question it works well for some couples, and that's great, but—and stay with me here—maybe, just maybe, not all infidelities are worth ending an otherwise good relationship over. Making sexual monogamy *the* barometer of a successful relationship, for everyone, might be like throwing out an otherwise perfect apple because it has one brown spot on it. Maybe a little whoopee on the side should be . . . well, no big whoop rather than a deal breaker.

Plenty of people dismiss Savage's point of view as, um, *gay*, as if sleeping with more than one person is just what gay men do, while for more "moral" heterosexuals it's a sign of spiritual and personal weakness. But maybe we think that simply because we've been taught to think it, in the same way that not very long ago many people were taught that blacks were intellectually inferior or Jews were unscrupulous—and they actually believed it. Maybe when a relationship implodes over sexual infidelity, you're letting it do so in deference to what our culture has taught you, not because it has to.

Into the Lab

Science often responds to culture, so it's no accident that many a Ph.D. has made a study of monogamy, in essence hitching a ride on what is more or less a massive cultural conundrum.

Lab experiments indicate that three chemicals—oxytocin, dopamine, and vasopressin—make animals monogamous, but thus far the only animal that some of these experiments indicate is *maybe* across-the-board sexually faithful is the prairie vole, which usually mates with just one partner. When these chemicals were blocked in prairie voles, though, they got a little loving on the side, same as most other animals. But higher levels of oxytocin and vasopressin are only half of the equation. An animal also needs the *receptors* for the chemicals in order to be sexually monogamous, as indicated by a study on the montane vole, a species more inclined toward free love, that still screwed around when injected with oxytocin and vasopressin; unlike their flatlander cousins, montane voles don't have the receptors for the chemicals.

Scientists know that humans have both the chemicals and the receptors for monogamous behavior, but these can vary widely from individual to individual in terms of how many receptors they have and where exactly they are housed. To put it bluntly, some people just might be better than others at being sexually faithful, not just because they have little appetite for deceit or they unquestioningly honor their commitment to one person, but because of how their brains are wired. It follows, then, that variation among individuals, not monogamy or promiscuity for our whole species, is what's natural.

Much as our culture teaches us that monogamy is the only natural way among humans, it also threatens us with the damnation of unhappiness should we stray. Polyamory, we're instructed, only wreaks havoc and makes everyone involved deeply unhappy. But yet again, data just might prove this assumption wrong: In a twenty-year-long study of 164 couples, half of whom were monogamous and half of whom were not, Dr. Arline Rubin, a specialist in family studies, found that monogamy was by no means an indicator of happiness, nor was there any difference, in terms of the rate of splitting up, between monogamous and non-monogamous couples. In other words, whether one sleeps with other people outside a long-term relationship has nothing to do in the end with how stable the relationship is or how happy it is. Key to this data, however, is that the nonmonogamous couples were transparent about their status, and likely a similar survey of people who "cheated"—got some play on the side without negotiating for it— would yield very different results.

There's no doubt that nonmonogamy is scary stuff for many of us, and for good reason. But that said, it's worth exploring the difference between what's scary because you've been taught that it's dangerous and what's scary because of what you've learned from personal experience.

Detachment Theory

The Sound of It Is Something Quite Atrocious

Wʜɪʟᴇ ᴍᴏsᴛ ᴏꜰ us are charmed by the literally flighty main character in *Mary Poppins* and the hapless London family she tends to, a modern psychologist reading the classic story might come to a very different conclusion. With caretakers coming and going and parents who are distant and distracted, it could be read as a textbook case of *Childrearing: What Not to Do*. Were one to fast-forward twenty years to the adult Jane and Michael Banks, you might well find two individuals repeatedly banging their heads against the mysterious something that keeps them from being secure in their intimate relationships.

That's because these days what's known in professional circles as attachment theory is firmly entrenched in our notions of what children—and adults—need in order to lead stable, emotionally fulfilling lives. Whether you're aware of it, the moment you sit down in therapy with your latte to deconstruct (yet again!) how your relationship with your parents strangely parallels your romantic disappointments, you are chewing the cud of attachment theory.

John Bowlby: Poster Child for the Mary Poppins Paradigm Makes Good

Were it not for John Bowlby, a man so fascinated by the notion of separation that it dominated his entire career in the field of developmental psychology, we might well all be stuck in the distinctly unhelpful muck and mire of the id, ego, superego, oedipal complexes, oral stages, and, my personal favorite, penis envy. Freud might have invented the fifty-minute session, but what we talk about in those fifty minutes now—indeed, what we talk about when we talk about love within the confines of our therapists' offices—we owe to John Bowlby.

In 1920s England the dominant thinking among psychiatric circles was that all neuroses were rooted in sexuality and repression. To many of those following in Freud's footsteps, a child who wailed for a missing parent was merely immature, and for a child who was delinquent, neurotic, or just plain difficult the best treatment was to "emancipate" that child from his or her mother. But even as a young man fresh out of university, while working at a school for "maladjusted" children, Bowlby saw the elephant in the living room of British society: that British (and psychoanalytic) notions of what was good for young children—namely, separating them from their parents—was creating generation after generation of emotional cripples.

Bowlby's sensitivity to children separated from their parents must have been informed by his own family history and place in upper-middle-class society, the details of which are fleshed out in a biography of his early life by Suzan van Dijken. He was one of six children, all of whom were brought up by a nanny and nursemaids in the Mary Poppins paradigm. Their days were strictly regimented—meals, sleep, play, and lessons all in the attic nursery, a once-daily outing to Hyde Park, an hour visiting their mother in the drawing room in the late afternoon. Significantly, Bowlby was deeply attached to one nursemaid, Minnie, who left her post when he was under the age of four. The children barely saw their father, a private physician to King George V. In 1914, when World War I broke out, his father left for the French front; several years later, when John was eleven, he and his brother were sent to a boarding school to keep them safe from air raids—and because boarding school was simply what people of a certain class did with one's children. It's likely that John didn't see his father for months or even years at a time during the war.

After studying psychology at Cambridge, Bowlby was drawn to what we would now label "at-risk" children. He started to put two and two together in a way that no one else in his field had yet: Separate a child from his or her mother and there will be, one way or another, hell to pay, in the form of delinquency, kleptomania, lack of affection, or general emotional problems. For the next few years, Bowlby tried to find his way in a field where his colleagues were looking so hard at the meaning of fantasy that they forgot the meaning of reality: that it was a cultural norm for children in the upper classes to grow up with remote parental figures and caregivers who, like Bowlby's own beloved Minnie, could come and go.

Operation Pied Piper and the Unstable Young Adult

In one, Piggy goes splat; in the other, tea with Mr. Tumnus. Surely no two books could have less in common than *Lord of the Flies* and *The Lion, the Witch and the Wardrobe,* right? But the two classics actually do share a fair number of similarities: Each novel explores what happens when children are left to their own devices, but, more pertinent to our discussion, each plot is set in motion when children are evacuated from war zones. Both are reflections on the very real, very British experience of what was known as Operation

Pied Piper, a World War II policy deployed by the Ministry of Health to protect children from German bombings. In just four days in September 1939, 2 million children, gas masks in hand, waved teary good-byes to their parents, and were dispatched to live with strangers in the lightly populated countryside.

Protecting children from German bombs was, of course, a noble intention. But it had once been the case that only the upper classes put their children on train platforms and sent them away; now much of England, regardless of social station, was doing it. With the advent of Operation Pied Piper and in effect the dissolution of class distinctions in familial separation practices, Bowlby, who had been quietly refining his ideas about the importance of a stable, loving attachment between mother and child, raised a red flag. Just a few months after the first evacuation, he published a paper in the *British Medical Journal* in which he vigorously critiqued the policy, warning that, particularly for children between the ages of two and five, evacuation would result in "very serious and widespread psychological disorder" and, a decade down the road, a spike in juvenile delinquency. Children at that age, he argued, could interpret separation from their families in only one way: that they were unwanted.

After World War II, Bowlby's career gathered steam when he was able to actually study how personality development was affected when young children were separated from their mothers. If a child has a happy, healthy relationship with his mother and other family members, Bowlby wrote in 1948, "we believe there is every likelihood that the child will be able to develop similar satisfactory relationships in later life with people outside the immediate circle of his family; conversely, if this relationship develops adversely, we believe that he will probably become disturbed emotionally to a greater or lesser degree, and may be confronted throughout his life by difficulties in his personal relationships." Of course, these days this is obvious stuff, but then, in a society where separating children from their parents had long been an indicator of wealth and prestige and therapists advocated for splitting up troubled families rather than treating them and keeping them together, it wasn't.

Attachment Theory: The Great Leap Forward

In 1949 the World Health Organization commissioned Bowlby to write a report on homeless children. The result, *Maternal Care and Mental Health*, was widely circulated, and in it his conclusion was unequivocal: "Prolonged deprivation of the young child of maternal care may have grave and far-reaching effects on his character . . . the whole of his future life." Again, things that we take for granted now, like the vicious circle in which deprived children grow up to be deficient parents, who in turn raise deprived children, and that parentless children should be adopted or placed in loving foster homes rather than in group care as soon after birth as possible, were in his report. No one had put it all together before.

With the incredible success of *Maternal Care and Mental Health* (four hundred thousand copies sold in English, and it was translated into fourteen other languages!), Bowlby had become one of the most influential social critics of his time. But much as he'd launched a legacy, he still lacked a cohesive theory that really explained *why* infants object so to being separated from their mothers.

Bowlby was onto a few things: first, that classic Freudianism had some weak points that were ripe for debunking and, second, that additional data was necessary to support the notion that in order to become normal, stable adults, infants and young children need an intimate, stable relationship with at least one primary caregiver. To make the leap from the myopia of Freudianism, Bowlby knew he needed to intensively study not just psychology but evolution and animal behavior as well.

Between 1958 and 1960, he published three now-classic papers that helped build his body of research, and in 1969 he published *Attachment*, the first volume in what became a trilogy called *Attachment and Loss*. Attachment theory, decades in the making, finally had a name. It explained how relationships form and dissolve, and it took the emotions into account, as well as physiology, cognition, behavior, and, most important, evolution. At its core, attachment theory explains how mammals survive: We are social creatures, dependent on one another, and without connection behaviors like looking, following, cuddling, and comforting, we die. The more contact and connection you have with your caregivers, the more likely you are to survive.

> "Limerence," a term psychologists often use, was coined in 1977 to describe the obsessive state of mind that can accompany intense romantic love. Under the influence of limerence, an individual might feel downright desperate to have their feelings reciprocated, and overcome by doubt, hope, and what one might call lovesickness.

Bowlby built the platform, but one of his colleagues in developmental psychology, Mary Ainsworth, did the research and coined the terms that are now used to categorize attachment patterns in infants: *secure* (children who when in a strange situation seek comfort from their mothers, are calmed easily, and then resume playing or exploring), *avoidant* (children who seem unmoved when their primary caregiver comes or goes), and *ambivalent/resistant/anxious* (children who remain distressed by separation from their caregiver and won't be calmed by a stranger). Just as important, she noted that there was a connection between how sensitive and responsive the parent was to the child and how secure the child was in his or her attachment.

As attachment theory swept through psychology in the 1970s, the connections between infant behavior patterns and adult behavior patterns in close romantic relationships were hard to miss: the sense of safety, the hugging and kissing, the "I'd do anything for you," even the cooing "baby talk." Could it be, then, that on some levels romantic attachments were not so different from attachments between children and their caregivers? In the mid-1980s, leading developmental psychologists had concluded not only that while genetics and later experience play a role, how one connects to a caregiver as an infant can profoundly affect how you connect with people later on, but also that adult attachment came in four flavors that riffed on those established by Ainsworth:

- secure ("Being close is easy! I don't worry much about being alone or not being accepted.")
- anxious-preoccupied ("I want to be emotionally intimate with people, but they don't want to be with me!)
- dismissive-avoidant ("I'd rather not depend on others or have others depend on me!")
- fearful-avoidant ("I want to be close, but what if I get hurt?")

If you're anything like me, these categories sure explain a hell of a lot, not just in terms of myself but with respect to men I've loved and even close friends.

Taking Charge

So if the hydra-headed attachment theory is a valid (if broad) explanation for how close relationships function and why we suffer so much when our connection with a loved one is severed—and why in therapy you hear an internal *ding! ding! ding!* when you finally put it together that there might be a connection between, say, the fact that your mother was severely depressed when you were a young child and your own difficulty operating intimate relationships as an adult—the questions then become: Are attachment patterns stable over time? Can you change? Once avoidant, always avoidant; once anxious, always anxious? Can a needy person ever become a secure one?

The good news is: Maybe. The latest thinking indicates that while there is some overlap between how you connected with your mother as an infant and how you connect with your romantic partners as an adult, it's not immutable. People can assimilate new information, and that information can alter their levels or patterns of attachment in time. I like to think of it this way: Over the course of the multiple intimate relationships that many of us have in our adult lives, we constantly acquire new information that we can fold like meringue into the stiffer batter of what has gone before.

In other words, while you can't teach an old dog new tricks, he might just be able to teach himself. Let's say, for example, you've spent your entire twenties "anxiously attached" to romantic partners—sitting by the phone, waiting for texts, wondering when the other shoe will drop and he'll dump you, and so on—chances are you know that your anxiety makes you miserable. But if you examine your attachment style and come to understand others, with hard work you can learn to shift your attention to love interests who don't make you feel like you're constantly waiting and quite simply never getting enough. John Bowlby has been dead now for over twenty years, but if he were alive to see you make that transformation, he just might be first to issue you a hearty "Righto!"

Addicted to Love

As far as we know, the body's earliest explorers were the ancient Greeks, who established protocols for dissection and vivisection that formed the basis of medical knowledge and practice for centuries. At their core, however, these explorations were as much about attempting to understand humans' emotional lives as they were hazarding guesses about bodily mechanics. And much as some of their conclusions may strike us as ridiculous now, like Aristotle's claim that the heart was an intelligent organ and the seat of emotion, thanks to modern science we know that he was onto something: Tissues deep in our bodies can explain inner life. To put it simply, cells can explain sadness.

For years exploration into the workings of the human brain was invasive and confined to autopsies and horrible experiments we need not cover here, but in recent decades technology has made it increasingly possible to learn about the brain without ever really touching it.

Since the mid-1990s or so, inquiring minds have turned to functional magnetic resonance imaging (fMRI) machines to learn just what happens in our brains. Simply by passing a person through the machine, which looks a bit like a gigantic doughnut, scientists can use an fMRI to measure changes in blood flow in the brain, thereby mapping neural activity. The fields of medicine, biology, and psychology are inundated with fMRI studies that have dramatically expanded knowledge about the chemical and physiological mechanisms that underpin human behavior.

This Is Your Brain in Love

The earliest pairings of fMRI scanning and love research, from around 2005, and led by psychologist Art Aron, neurologist Lucy Brown, and anthropologist Helen Fisher, established the baseline that would inform research going forward: what a brain in love looks like. When individuals who were deeply in love viewed images of their beloved and simultaneously had their brains scanned, the vivid casts of yellows, greens, and blues—fireworks across gray matter—clearly showed that romantic love activates in the caudate nucleus, via a flood of dopamine.

The caudate nucleus is associated with what psychologists call "motivation and goal-oriented behavior," or "the rewards system." To many of these experts, the fact that love fires there suggests that love isn't so much an emotion in its own right— although aspects of it are obviously highly emotional—as it is a "goal-oriented motivational state." (When you stop to think about that in terms of facial expressions and how emotions pass over our countenances, that makes sense. Emotions are characterized by particular, passing facial expressions—a frown with anger, a smile with happiness, an open mouth with shock—while if you had to identify the face of someone "in love," it would be harder to do, and love isn't a reaction that passes in a matter of minutes or hours.) It follows, then, that as far as brain wiring is concerned, romantic love is the motivation to obtain and retain the object of your affections.

But an episode steeped in romantic love, like an afternoon spent alone with your beloved, isn't the only thing that triggers the motivation to obtain and retain or stimulates increases in dopamine and its rocketlike path through your reward system. Nicotine and cocaine follow exactly the same pattern: Smoke a cigarette, dopamine is released, the feeling is pleasant, and you want more. Snort a line of coke, dopamine is released, the feeling is awesome, and you want more. Partake and you are in a "goal-oriented motivational state." Take this to its logical conclusion and, as far as brain wiring is concerned, when you're in love, it's not *as if* you're an addict. You *are* an addict.

This Is Your Brain on Heartbreak

As most of us know all too well, when you're reeling from the finale of a romantic relationship that you didn't want to come to a close, your emotional and bodily reactions are a tangle: You're still in love and want to reconcile, but you're also angry and confused; simultaneously, you're jonesing for a "fix" of the person who has abruptly left your life, and you might go to dramatic, even embarrassing, lengths to get it, even though part of you knows better.

Just as love at its best is explained by fMRI scans, so, too, is love at its worst. In 2010 the team who first used fMRI scanning to establish the connection between love and the caudate nucleus and saw what happy romantic love looks like set out to see what it looks like when love wrecks and confusion, anger, and hurt feelings enter the mix. They gathered a group of individuals who were in the first stages of a breakup, all of whom reported that they thought about their rejecter approximately 85 percent of their waking hours and yearned to reunite with their rejecter. Moreover, all of these lovelorn reported "signs of lack of emotion control on a regular basis since the initial breakup, occurring regularly for weeks or months. This included inappropriate phoning, writing or e-mailing, pleading for reconciliation, sobbing for hours, drinking too much and/or making dramatic entrances and exits into the rejecter's home, place of work or social space to express anger, despair or passionate love." In other words, each of these bereft souls had it *bad*.

Then, with appropriate controls, the researchers passed their subjects through fMRI machines, where they could look at photographs of their beloved (called the "rejecter stimulus"), and simultaneously prompted them to share their feelings and experience, which elicited statements such as "It hurt so much," "I don't want to break up until I have exhausted every possibility of getting back together," and "I hate what he/she did to me."

A few particularly interesting patterns in brain activity emerged:

As far as the midbrain reward system is concerned, they were still "in love." Just because the "reward" is delayed in coming (or, more to the point, not coming at all), that doesn't mean the neurons that are expecting "reward" shut down. They keep going and going, waiting and waiting for a "fix." Not surprisingly, among the experiment's subjects, the caudate was still very much in love and reacted in an almost Pavlovian way to the image of the loved one. Even though cognitively they knew that their relationships were over, part of each participant's brain was still in anticipation mode. Moreover, the researchers speculated, because this particular area that activates in the brain is also associated with "reward evaluation," they were still learning, madly assessing the situation, and adjusting their behavior. In other words, they were still *motivated* by their ex.

Parts of the brain were trying to override others. The orbital frontal cortex, which is involved in learning from emotions and controlling behavior, activated. As we all know, when you're in the throes of heartbreak, you want to do things you'll probably regret later, but at the same time another part of you is trying to keep a lid on it.

They were still addicted. As they viewed images of their reject-ers, regions of the brain that typically fire in individuals craving and addicted to drugs were activated. Again, no different from someone addicted to—and attempting a withdrawal from—nicotine or cocaine.

While these conclusions explain in broad strokes what happens in our brains when we're dumped, one expert on attachment I turned to, Phillip Shaver of the University of California, Davis, described what happens in our breakup brains in a slightly differ-ent way: "In the case of a lost love, if the relationship went on for a long time, the grieving person has thousands of neural circuits de-voted to the lost person, and each of these has to be brought up and reconstructed to take into account the person's absence. This can be both surprising and very painful. . . . Each representational cir-cuit has to be revised to acknowledge the person's absence."

Which brings us, of course, to the pain.

♥ The Miss Havisham Effect

For some people, grief itself can be addictive. In 2008, researchers at the University of California, Los Angeles, showed that people suffering from what's called "complicated grief"—mourning that in essence gets stuck rather than alleviating over time—have elevated activity in the brain systems associated with rewards and attachment. Every time people suffering from complicated grief see a cue reminding them of their lost loved one, because the requisite neurons haven't fully integrated the information that the person is gone, their brain continues to expect a reward. The researchers coined the phenomenon the "Miss Havisham effect" after the jilted bride in the novel *Great Expectations*. (See page 207.)

The Sensation

When you're deep in the mire of heartbreak, chances are that you feel pain somewhere in your body—probably in your chest or stomach. Some people describe it as a dull ache, others as piercing, while still others experience it as a crushing sensation. The pain can last for a few seconds and then subside, or it can be chronic, hanging over your days and depleting you like just like the pain, say, of a back injury or a migraine.

But how can we reconcile the sensation of our hearts breaking—when in fact they don't, at least not literally—with biophysical reality? What actually *happens* in our bodies to create that sensation? The short answer is that no one knows. The long answer is that the pain might be caused by the simultaneous hormonal triggering of the *sympathetic activation system* (most commonly referred to as fight-or-flight stress that ramps up heart and lung action) and the *parasympathetic activation system* (known as the rest-and-digest response, which slows the heart down and is tied to the social-engagement system). In effect, then, it could be as if the heart's accelerator and brakes are pushed simultaneously, and those conflicting actions create the sensation of heartbreak.

While no one has as of yet been able to study what exactly goes on in the upper-body cavity during moments of acutely felt heartbreak that might account for the physical pain, the results of the earlier-mentioned fMRI study of the responses of heartbroken individuals indicated that when the subjects looked at and discussed their rejecter, they trembled, cried, sighed, and got angry, and in their brains these emotions triggered activity in the same area associated with physical pain. Another study that explored the emotional/physical pain connection compared fMRI results on subjects who touched a hot probe with those who looked at a photo of an ex-partner and mentally relived that particular experience of rejection. The results confirmed that social rejection and physical pain are rooted in exactly the same regions of the brain, so when you say you're "hurt" as a result of being rejected by someone close to you, you're not just leaning on a metaphor. As far as your brain is concerned, the pain you feel is no different from a stab wound.

This neatly parallels the discoveries made that indicate that love can be addictive on a par with cocaine and nicotine. Much as we think of "heartbreak" as a verbal expression of our pain or say we "can't quit" someone, these are not actually artificial constructs—they are rooted in physical realities. How wonderful that science, and specifically images of our brains, should reveal that metaphors aren't poetic flights of fancy. In some way that we have yet to fully fathom, language expresses invisible bodily realities.

But it's important to note here that heartbreak falls under the rubric of what psychologists who specialize in pain call "social pain"—the activation of pain in response to the loss of or threats to social connection. From an evolutionary perspective, the "social pain" of separation likely served a purpose back on the savannas that were the hunting and gathering grounds of our ancestors. There, safety relied on numbers; exclusion of any kind, including separation from a group or one's mate, signaled death, just as physical pain could signal a life-threatening injury. Psychologists reason that the neural circuitries of physical pain and emotional pain evolved to share the same pathways to alert proto-humans to danger; physical and emotional pain, when saber-toothed tigers lurked in the brush, were cues to pay close attention or risk death.

On the surface that functionality wouldn't seem terribly relevant now—after all, few of us risk attack by a wild animal charging at us from behind the lilacs at any given moment, and living alone doesn't mean a slow, lonely death. But still, the pain is there to teach us something. It focuses our attention on significant social events and forces us to learn, correct, avoid, and move on.

When you look at social pain from this perspective, you have to acknowledge that in our society we're often encouraged to hide it. We bottle it up. While of course it's possible to be private about one's pain and still deal with it, if you're totally ignoring it and the survival theory holds true, then you're putting yourself at risk because you're not alerting others that there is a crisis.

The Great Conundrum

Several studies, also using the hot probe + image + fMRI combo, have shown that looking at an image of a loved one actually reduces the experience of physical pain, in much the same way that, say, holding a loved one's hand during a frightening or painful procedure does, or kissing a child's boo-boo makes the tears go away. Science shows that love is effectively a painkiller, because it activates the same sections of brain stimulated by morphine and cocaine; moreover, the effects are actually quite strong.

On one level this suggests a wonderfully simple and elegant solution, albeit a New Agey one, to physical or emotional pain: All you need is love. And it bolsters the notion, faulty for some of us though it may be, that if you're suffering from a broken heart, moving on fast can bring relief.

Whether or not you move on quickly to someone new is possibly rooted in your attachment style. (See page 92.) While some of us need a little time-out after a breakup, one study by a Canadian team of psychologists showed that for "anxiously attached" individuals a rebound relationship can be just the ticket to restore their optimism and help them get over an ex. The researchers maintained that it's not so much the rebound relationship itself that gets an anxiously attached individual to move on from the past, but more the reassurance that there are other fish in the sea.

There's a point, however, where this trend in fMRI research starts to enter a prickly realm: Because physical pain and emotional pain—like heartbreak—travel along the same pathways in the brain, as covered earlier, this means that theoretically they can be *medically* treated in the same way. In fact, researchers from the University of Toronto recently showed that acetaminophen—yep, regular old Tylenol—reduces the experience of social pain. The report of their study states, "We have shown for the first time that acetaminophen, an over-the-counter medication commonly used to reduce physical pain, also reduces the pain of social rejection, at both neural and behavioral levels."

But some experts argue that the moment you put a toe on the slippery slope of popping pills to make you feel better emotionally, you have to wonder if doing so circumvents nature's plan. You're *supposed* to feel bad, to sit with it, to review what went wrong, even to the point of obsession, so that you learn your lesson and don't make the same mistake again.

And what does all this mean on a cultural level? While they might not admit it, for biologists and psychologists, understanding love on a chemical level is tantamount to finding the holy grail. After all, at least on a philosophical level, the more we understand about love in terms of science . . . well then, the closer we are to understanding what makes humans human, an advance that might be on a par with physicists cracking the mystery of the space-time continuum.

Ultimately, all this progress points to one thing: treatment, with both painkillers and antiaddiction drugs. Perhaps recovering from heartbreak could be as simple as wearing a patch (Lovaderm!) or chewing a special gum (Lovorette!) or popping a pill (Alove!) that just makes the pain go away.

If you could take a pill that assured that you could fall in love, fall out of love, or stay in love on command, would you take it? Would availing yourself of that kind of technology make you more human, simply because technology is by definition human, or less so?

· III ·

MUSIC AND ART

———————

Music

W HEN YOU'VE JUST been dumped, nothing feels as good as feeling worse, and music is often the thing that gets you there. Whether you torment yourself by playing a song that was the anthem of your love during happier times over and over again, turn to oldies but goodies from previous times of woe, or discover new tracks or albums that perfectly capture just how bad you feel, it's almost as if no heartbreak is complete without the right notes. When you're in that state, music sometimes seems like the only appropriate accessory to isolation. It "gets you" far better than any friend or relative. When you're looking for something to confirm that yes, you really are worse off without him, nothing hits the spot like precisely the right song.

I've always wondered if musicians make conscious choices about whether to be explicit or inexplicit about sad love or if it just tumbles out one way or the other or is simply determined by the type of music they write. Much of Johannes Brahms's work, for example, is either entirely instrumental or religious and choral, but that doesn't mean that certain pieces are not very much a reflection of his romantic disasters. Then there are the songs that never name names, like Carly Simon's "You're So Vain," which has for years been one of pop music's greatest mysteries. In recent music history, barely legal Taylor Swift has never denied that her song "Dear John" is about lothario John Mayer, and both of British soul sensation Adele's albums, *19* and *21*, have been heart-on-her-sleeve meditations on her own real-life breakups.

Sometimes we don't really want to know the stories behind the music—that can fog our own experience with it. But that is a fundamentally selfish approach; what happens behind the music, what creates it, is every bit as important as the music itself.

Franz Liszt

IF TALENT ALONE is an aphrodisiac, then Franz Liszt (1811–86) was a quadruple shot of hot: He was not only a phenomenal pianist and composer but also ferociously smart, extraordinarily handsome, and shockingly personable. "Nature," one friend commented, "seems to have done everything for him." It's not surprising, then, that he was one of music history's great heartbreakers.

While we have no recordings of a Liszt performance, he was often called the greatest pianist of all time by those who did hear him. As a young prodigy, he spent his early years performing in Hungary and Vienna; when he was twelve, his middle-class parents took their only child to Paris so he could play with the big boys, which he did with modesty and aplomb. Before Franzi could even shave, he'd been presented to royalty across Europe and had written an opera. When a contemporary critic wrote of him that he had "a prodigious fecundity, a miraculous digital dexterity which hold[s] his audience in ecstasy," no doubt aristocratic women from the Danube to the Thames sighed in anticipation over what kind of man this wunderkind would become. Their fantasies about him might well have been good indicators of not just what kind of lover he'd be but what kind of woman he'd love.

First Love, First Loss

Like many child prodigies who have yet to learn how to manage their talents, Franzi had an urge to rebel, which in his case meant flirting with the idea of chucking it all and becoming a priest. "I dreamed myself incessantly into the world of saints," he recalled many years later. But according to *The Young Liszt* by Iwo and Pamela Zaluski, his father, Adam, who had cultivated his son's talent from when he was just a tiny boy, argued that God-given gifts like his should not be abandoned for a mere priesthood. Upon Adam's death from typhoid when Franzi was just fifteen, Franz was suddenly the family's breadwinner. Teaching the sons and daughters of the idle rich was simply the best way to provide for his family.

He camped out in Paris and became a workaholic, running around the city from one student's home to another and, like any child superstar, fueling himself with tobacco and booze. But around 1828, by which point he was seventeen, the true perks of teaching revealed themselves in his demure young pupil Caroline de Saint-Cricq, the daughter of a count and minister of commerce to King Charles X. Caroline was "of angelic beauty, and [had] a complexion like a lily flushed with roses," Liszt told a close friend. While he introduced her to the fine points of interpreting music, she instilled in him a love of literature and started him down the path to becoming an autodidact of the first measure. Rather than vigorously object to the budding romance—as would be expected of a member of the aristocracy over a flirtation with a mere servant, which is what music teachers, no matter how brilliant and well known, were considered—her mother let them steal kisses and hold hands during the lessons she chaperoned. Likely she saw that Liszt's intelligence and piety were a good match for her daughter's.

But when Caroline's mother died suddenly, her father moved

quickly to remove Franzi from the scene. One night Franzi over-stayed his welcome, and shortly thereafter the comte summoned him, announced that Caroline would soon be marrying the comte d'Artigaux in the Pyrenees, and dismissed Franzi. In their last meeting, Caroline and Franzi pledged to think of each other three times every day when church bells rang for the Angelus call to prayer.

Caroline was so devastated that she became incredibly sick, and she begged her father to allow her to enter a nunnery rather than be forced into an arranged marriage. No go—she was dispatched to the south without further ado. As for Franzi, this heartbreak was enough to make him a virtual shut-in, and again he resolved to enter a seminary and become a priest. While this is hard to imagine in an otherwise healthy eighteen-year-old, his breakdown was described to be so brutal that he had lapses in consciousness and even seizures. One wonders what license was taken in these descriptions in the name of Romanticism, but it is true that his health declined to the point where a Parisian newspaper actually printed his obituary.

Caroline and Franzi saw each other only one more time in their lives, in 1844, when he toured in southern France, fifteen years into Caroline's unhappy marriage. According to Adrian Williams's *Portrait of Liszt*, in 1853 she wrote to him, "If the divine mercy would allow me to be able to press your hand, my heart would be open again for a few days. . . . I love you with all the power of my soul, and wish for you the happiness that I myself no longer know."

In keeping with the stereotype of the long-suffering artist, Franzi appears to have wallowed for a couple of years after the debacle with Caroline. Then, in the summer of 1830, the July Revolution hit France and Charles X was deposed in favor of a more populist government. A more liberal atmosphere gave what until then had just been the seeds of Romanticism the sunlight and water they needed to blossom into a full-fledged movement. Writers, artists, and musicians flocked from points east to Paris, and with Romanticism now officially in vogue, Franzi had a new lease on life.

Whether he was bolstered by a sense of finally belonging, or if he was "on the rebound," as we'd now call it, or if he'd at last found a way to reconcile his carnal impulses with his piety, a new chapter in Franzi's intimate life began—one in which he likely had flings with at least a few of the many rich and beautiful women who threw themselves at him. If Franz Liszt had a type, it was married and aristocratic. Among them was Adèle Laprunarède, a thirty-four-year-old comtesse who was married to a much older, indifferent count. With Adèle, Franzi experimented in what he cagily referred to as "exercises in the lofty French style"—particularly while snowed in with her at her castle in the Alps for an entire winter. (And by "lofty" one assumes he didn't mean the altitude.) The affair didn't last long, and its mysterious end was apparently unhappy, but it did confirm that what he'd started with Caroline would turn out to be a lifelong commitment to breaking class boundaries and creating scandal when it came to choosing his romantic mates.

Enter the Angel

In 1833, Liszt was still sifting through the rubble of the end of his affair with Adèle when he was invited to a musical gathering at a friend's home. There he met the twenty-seven-year-old comtesse Marie d'Agoult, an attractive (and once again married) woman who had long blond curls and tended to dress in cascades of tulle and muslin. ("Involuntarily," one of her contemporaries remembered of Marie, "one looked for her wings.") Marie hadn't wanted to go to the party that night at all—she was a serious, bookish sort who dreaded boring society conversation—but it seems that as soon as she saw Liszt, she knew she was in trouble. Years after that fateful night, she remembered their bracing first chat, as well as the fact that she didn't sleep well afterward.

The immediate chemistry between them was obvious, but now Marie's challenge was making the first move in a way that was appropriate to the differences in their stations. She struggled to find just the right words to invite him to visit her at home. Luckily, Marie lived mostly independently of her husband, so she and Franzi had the freedom and privacy to become fast friends. In Marie, expressive, sensitive Franzi found a sympathetic listener regarding his troubles with Adèle, and in Franzi, intellectually lonely Marie found someone who could talk about literature, progressive politics, and religion. What's more, they quickly found they shared common ground in that they were both unhappy, both embittered by their romantic experiences. In this meeting of two old souls, the mighty universe seemed to open up, and it threatened to swallow them whole.

Marie bought an estate in Croissy, outside of Paris, shortly after meeting Franzi, although whether or not it was to keep distance between herself and her young friend or to give them privacy and shelter is unclear. But before long she invited him to visit, and as soon as he arrived, the gravity of what they were embarking on was simultaneously crystal clear and unspeakable: "When he was shown into the salon, my children were there with me. He had never seen them before. . . . What passed suddenly through his mind at that moment? What thought went through it like an arrow? I do not know, but his beautiful face changed expression and his features contracted. For a moment neither of us was able to speak. Franz had stopped on the threshold. I took a few steps toward him, abashed and trembling. In the same lightning flash of conscience we had felt our guilt, or apparently so, for neither of us dared mention it." Before long they overcame their joint trepidation. Their next lovely weeks together were, of course, utterly enchanted—that magical, crazy time when you're falling in love and you've admitted it. Their relationship continued this way into 1834, both at Croissy and at a grungy apartment, which they called the *Ratzenloch*, or "rat hole," that Liszt rented in Paris for their secret rendezvous. "With Caroline I was merely a child; with Adèle only a wretched, fainthearted milksop. With you alone do I feel young and manly," he proclaimed to her.

Unmarried Bliss

As is so often the case with these stories, tragedy was waiting in the wings. In 1834, Marie's five-year-old daughter, Louise, died. For some people facing so great a loss, companionship is a balm, but Marie just wanted to be isolated with her anguish. Franzi knew her well enough to know that she needed to be left alone.

Shortly after reuniting a few months later, but while Marie was still in a fog of grief, she discovered she was pregnant. She was faced with the choice of bearing his child but not living with him openly or bucking the world she'd grown up in and living in sin with the man she loved. She decided on the latter, left her husband a note, and bolted for Switzerland, where Franzi met up with her. "All ties were broken off," Marie wrote, "rejected, kicked aside, except our love." As was the custom when a woman left her husband, she also left behind their surviving daughter.

The next months were effectively a working honeymoon, bun-in-the-oven style: Marie and Franzi lived in tiny villages in the Alps, where he read religious texts and composed some and she wrote as well.

While in Switzerland, Franzi wrote "Au Lac de Wallenstadt" for Marie, a piece that forever moved her to tears. It's evocative of the sound of waves and the paddling of oars—a great example of the notion of "program music" that Liszt supported. The aim of "program music" is to create a composition that evokes, say, a landscape—a sort of musical impressionism.

While on this idyll, they collaborated on essays that fused their political and artistic beliefs with their personal experience: Artists should not be regarded as servants but rather as esteemed members of the community. Slowly but surely they established themselves in the more modest and gentle Swiss social scene. Liszt introduced her to his friends and colleagues without shame, and she surprised society by acting like any other married woman rather than a pariah. One fellow aristocrat noted with shock that Marie "talked about Parisian society as though she were still a member of it." Again and again Marie managed to charm the doubters.

In December 1835 their daughter Blandine was born, and for the next few years they lived in itinerant bliss—often in semi-isolation in Switzerland and sometimes on the shores of Lake Como in Italy or back near Paris, where they stayed for months on end with their close friend, the scandalous novelist George Sand. It didn't take much to maintain their exquisite happiness—occasional concerts, a piano at home, good friends, writing and books.

♥ Film Alert!

Franz and Marie were part of a tight group of friends that included George Sand, Frédéric Chopin, and Eugène Delacroix. The 1991 film *Impromptu* chronicles the early days of the romance between George Sand and Chopin against the highly entertaining backdrop of the Romantic brat pack's shenanigans. Ignore the terrible accents and Hugh Grant's painful rendition of Chopin, as well as the liberties taken with each character, to just enjoy Bernadette Peters's interpretation of Marie as petulant and scheming, to the point of camp, and Julian Sands's passionate, chisel-cheekboned Liszt.

By 1838 the couple had a second daughter, Cosima, and Franzi had started to tour again, where packed houses marveled over his electrifying showmanship and downright acrobatic hands. One listener compared him to "a meteor."

Trouble in Paradise

In 1839, Marie had a third child, Daniel, and while observers noted that their mutual love and respect seemed to be unchanged, Marie was worn down by childbearing and by Franzi's lengthy absences. "You are too preoccupied with being great," she wrote him. "You are so strong that you take no account of the weakness of others. For you, everything is very simple. . . . You subsist arrogantly on the consciousness of your greatness and fail to appreciate the little sorrows of weaker souls."

Liszt's concert schedule was astonishing. During the period from about 1839 to 1847, he typically performed three to four times a week, so it wouldn't be an exaggeration to say that within eight years he performed over a thousand times. After 1842 his concerts were marked by "Lisztomania"—his female fans went wild, reaching states of mystical ecstasy during his performances and scrambling for any piece of him, anything he had touched or was associated with—his gloves or silk scarf, a lock of his hair, a broken piano string, even spent coffee grounds or cigar butts. Nearly 150 years after his death, there's even a song by the band Phoenix called "Lisztomania."

Superstar that Franz was, he also frequently performed to support a number of charitable causes, from the construction of the Beethoven monument to aid for the thousands left homeless by the Great Fire of Hamburg in 1842. He was also keen on what we would now call art therapy and was known to visit prisons and hospitals to share music with inmates and patients.

But more to the point, it seems that while on the road her Franzi had developed a taste for philandering—including, reportedly, with Irish actress and aristocrat Lola Montez, and he wasn't exactly discreet about it. "I'm willing to be your mistress, but not one of your mistresses," Marie warned him. The vulgarity of his womanizing appalled her.

Franzi was still deeply attached to Marie and to their family life, but Marie insisted that they call it quits. It took several years to make the break, but in 1844, after eleven years together, they were done. Tragically for Marie, this meant losing her children yet again (fathers always assumed custody), and nine-year-old Blandine, seven-year-old Cosima, and five-year-old Daniel were sent off to Franzi's mother and saw very little of their own for the rest of their childhoods.

Franzi wasted no time moving on. Pretty immediately he took

up with his longtime friend Princess Belgiojoso (Balzac noted that at her house Liszt behaved liked the master); after that he took up with the celebrated French courtesan Marie Duplessis. Marie d'Agoult, meanwhile, took to gossiping about him and wrote him letters taunting him with his "failures," though it's hard to imagine what those were. They continued to torment each other in dispatches. "We used both of us to be noble creatures," he wrote her in 1846, "and you have cursed me, and I have banished myself from your heart because you misunderstood mine."

Marie once wrote that her own friends described her as six inches of snow covering twenty feet of lava. Sure enough, in 1846, she unleashed the lava. *Nélida* was her roman à clef, one of whose main characters was a composer struggling with the mismatch between his aggressive ambition and his mediocre talent. The blow was so low—and so ridiculous—that Liszt simply refused to be offended, even when everyone read it and asked him about it. "Rise above, rise above" was clearly his mantra, while "Hell hath no fury" was hers.

> During the nineteenth century, the roman à clef was a favored form of vengeance for any number of educated women, and just as Marie wrote one, she was bitten in the ass by another. So the story goes, when Marie said spiteful things about her friend George Sand to a mutual friend and Sand found out about it, she in turn supplied her friend Honoré de Balzac, the novelist, with details about Marie. Balzac then wrote *Béatrix*, which stars a character who bears an unflattering resemblance to Marie.

In the early 1860s, Franz and Marie's son, Daniel, and daughter Blandine both died. Right around then, likely in response to their children's deaths, Franz paid a visit to Marie. By that point Liszt was retired and had taken up with another woman, a fabulously rich Russian princess named Carolyne von Sayn-Wittgenstein, while Marie remained single. By Marie's account, though, she and Liszt were cordial, even linking arms and joining hands as they talked about their children. "Who would ever have said that we would meet again like this. That is at once sad and sweet. Above all, it cuts things human down to size: the great passions, the great sorrows, the great ambitions that rend and tear," she wrote in her journal. After he left, she couldn't stop thinking about the powerful bond that they still shared, more than twenty years after they split. Despite this touching reconciliation, she couldn't resist republishing her novel, and she went on to write her memoirs, which were published in 1877 after her death. She was buried in Père Lachaise near her friends and enemies Chopin, Delacroix, and Balzac. Doubtless Marie would be pleased as punch that nearly two hundred years after their electric first encounter, the details of how one of the world's greatest musicians broke her heart still fascinates.

The Nomad

Joni Mitchell's *Blue* is the quintessential breakup album, and for anyone who has ever been intimate with it, it will never have a successor. Although it was first released in 1971, it's an enduring darling of the critics—it made *Rolling Stone*'s 2003 list of the 500 Greatest Albums of All Time (the highest rank for an album by a woman in that particular list), sandwiched between Led Zeppelin's debut album and Bob Dylan's *Bringing It All Back Home*. In 2006, *Time* named it one of the most influential albums since 1954.

Joni wrote *Blue* in the receding waters of her breakup with Graham Nash of Crosby, Stills & Nash fame, mostly while traveling in Europe, and when it was recorded, it was done so in almost total privacy, with the doors locked and only the backup musicians allowed in. The sheer vulnerability in *Blue* reportedly moved Joni's friend Kris Kristofferson to beg of her, "Please! Leave something of yourself!" Mitchell has compared herself to cellophane during that period.

When I first started listening to *Blue* at about the age of ten, of course I had little understanding of the lyrics, but I still was in awe of what even my naïve brain recognized as her declaration of things deeply sad, private, and beautiful. It was my introduction to the sound of adult grief. By the time I was in my early twenties, the notion of guzzling a case of anyone made sense, and now the aspect of the album that hangs with me the most is the desperate, unsuccessful escapism—skating away on rivers, flying away on planes, sailing away, cloistering oneself on islands—the notion of being anywhere but here when your heart is broken. Licking one's wounds requires exquisite privacy. In *Blue*, Joni shows us how it's really done.

Some of my favorite breakup albums:

Eyes Open, Snow Patrol
Only the Lonely, Frank Sinatra
Face Value, Phil Collins
XO, Elliott Smith
The Boatman's Call, Nick Cave
Shoot Out the Lights, Richard and Linda Thompson
21, Adele

In the Air Tonight

THERE ARE OCCASIONS when a song is so good yet so mysterious that entire myths are built around it that obfuscate its true meaning. Such is the case with Phil Collins's song "In the Air Tonight," the key line being "Well, if you told me you were drowning / I would not lend a hand." Not long after the song was released, it seems some enterprising soul out there took it upon himself to concoct and spread the story that Phil had once stood helpless on a cliff and witnessed a friend drown while another man who was close enough to help stood idly by. According to the story, years passed and Phil wrote the song about the experience and sent the man who'd stood by a ticket for the front row at the show at which he'd premiere the song; the spotlight rested on the man in the front row as Phil sang it to him, while the man sat shattered in humiliation.

This story is, of course, utter hogwash, and it makes one wonder if every time Phil hears reference to it, he wants to laugh or cry. In keeping with the entire album, *Face Value*, the song is about Phil's split from his first wife, Andrea Bertorelli, whom he divorced in 1981 after she embarked on an affair with the couple's interior decorator.

Much as this particular song was gravely misinterpreted, Phil is still regarded as a master of the heartbreak song, so much so that he had a cameo role in a particularly wonderful episode (339, "Break-Up") of the radio program *This American Life*, in which he offers tips to a heartbroken young woman on how to write a love song. Phil is so wonderfully down to earth in it that you forget he's a kajillionaire and you quite want to give him a big hug. The piece pays homage not just to "Dr. Phil" but to Foreigner, the Magnetic Fields, Bonnie Raitt, and Dusty Springfield.

Johannes Brahms and Clara Schumann

If ever a relationship earned the reductionist "it's complicated," it would be that between celebrity pianist Clara Schumann (1819–96) and star composer Johannes Brahms (1833–97). For over forty years, Clara and Johannes went through the emotional gamut: They loved each other wildly, came to each other's rescue in times of horrific crisis, dumped salt in each other's wounds, and bickered like an old married couple, over and over and over. Against the backdrop of the agonies and ecstasies of nineteenth-century Romanticism and all the period's attendant madness and brilliance, these two were as emotionally intimate as two people can be.

There are times when walking through a door quite literally changes the course of one's life. Such was the case when twenty-year-old Brahms showed up at Clara and Robert Schumann's home in Düsseldorf in the fall of 1853. It was a moment worth imagining in detail: Brahms, a blond, barrel-chested, and handsome young man with bright blue eyes, awkward and likely a bit shabby, having just wrapped up a hiking trip, meeting Robert Schumann, who answered the door in his robe and slippers and would have had to gather his scattered thoughts to remember, "Ah, yes! This is the fellow I've heard about." Together they went to the parlor, where Schumann invited Brahms to sit down at his own piano, the one where he himself composed, to play. A few minutes into the young man's performance of his Piano Sonata no. 1 in C Major, Schumann stopped him; he had to call his wife, Clara, a semiretired piano prodigy, to witness the brilliance that was Brahms.

Surely Clara's presence made Brahms sweat bullets if he wasn't already. He'd toured as a pianist for only a year or so, and as a young boy he'd supported his family by playing the piano in his hometown of Hamburg's seediest brothels and dance halls (think sailors and St. Pauli girls). Suddenly here he was playing his own work for the period's musical power couple. That night Clara noted in her journal that Brahms played "as if sent from God," while Robert noted in his, "Visit from Brahms (a genius)."

According to Jan Swafford's biography of the composer, almost overnight Brahms was tucked into the bosom of the Schumann family—the three adults shared music, reading, and playing games in the cozy home, and Brahms became a favorite rambunctious playmate to the six Schumann children. Within days Robert was going to bat for Brahms professionally, contacting music publishers, penning commentaries, heralding the arrival of the new prodigy, introducing him to his friends. Brahms composed at a furious pace and honed his playing with Clara coaching him.

It was undoubtedly an idyllic time, particularly for Brahms, and he was an unexpected beacon for the Schumanns when darkness was falling fast. Clara, who was thirty-four at this point (fourteen years older than Brahms), had just discovered that she was expecting—possibly her tenth pregnancy in thirteen years of marriage. She was dispirited by the prospect of yet another child, but it came at an especially unfortunate time, as Robert's health was failing. They'd loved each other passionately and been professional collaborators since she was a teenager, but Robert suffered from what we would now call psychosis and was in and out of mental institutions often while they toured together. (Some scholars maintain that his psychosis was a symptom of syphilis rather than schizophrenia.)

By the time Brahms came into their lives that fall, Robert's uneven health meant bouts of mania and irritability, but within a few months Robert had gone off the deep end: Rational thought was chased away by "superhuman" orchestras that blasted in his head nonstop, and he said angels sang to him. One day in February 1854, Robert escaped from the house, again in his customary robe and slippers, and threw himself into the Rhine—a scene one can imagine as particularly surreal since it happened during carnival and his awful jump was witnessed by masked revelers.

Fishermen pulled Robert out of the river, and he was immediately whisked off to a mental hospital. While Robert stayed at the asylum, so ill he couldn't even say Clara's name, Brahms moved into the Schumann house, where he and Clara worked and waited in anguish. Brahms composed at a furious pace, and she, amazingly, had the energy to critique him.

♥ Book Alert!

For someone like me, who barely knows the difference between an F major and an F-bomb, the prospect of reading Jan Swafford's seven-hundred-plus-page *Johannes Brahms: A Biography* was one of the most daunting tasks to face. But I fell in love with this incredibly tender, thoughtful, and accessible work. Some passages were so precisely rendered, and I'd grown so attached to the personalities, that I literally read and wept.

Imagine for a moment these two personalities, locked in a vigil that had no end. On the one hand, Clara, who was serious and exacting. Her reputation as a virtuoso performer naturally carried over into her personal life, and at home she ran a tight ship. She was also a depressive sort—even when not in the midst of a crisis as grave as her husband's illness, she was prone to melancholy. On the other hand, Brahms, who with his mercurial personality could be impish and playful or abrupt, gruff, and tactless. Clara surely dressed meticulously, but Brahms was a bit of a slob and was known for not wearing socks.

Despite their differences in maturity and style, Clara relied on Brahms, recognizing that he was her rock. "That good Brahms always shows himself a most sympathetic friend. He does not say much, but one can see in his face, in his speaking eye, how he grieves with me," she wrote.

Brahms meanwhile was falling in love. In a letter—one of the few of his to survive—he shared with a friend that he felt as though he was under her spell. "I often have to restrain myself forcibly from just quietly putting my arms around her and even—I don't know, it seems to me so natural that she could not misunderstand," he wrote. As his biographer Jan Swafford notes, he was "living in an agony of frustrated desire. He wanted Schumann to get well; he wanted him to die." Brahms was navigating the treacherous waters of falling for a damsel in distress who was married and whose husband he loved and owed everything to.

In order to bring in some much-needed cash, Clara took up touring again, while twenty-two-year-old Brahms stayed at home with her children and assumed the role of deputy parent. And while Robert's doctors requested that Clara not visit her husband for fear that it would only make matters worse, Brahms was allowed to visit the sanatorium. Brahms saw his mentor drift in and out of lucidity, at some points well enough to write a letter, at other times unresponsive, at still others reduced to incoherent babbling. Out on the road, Clara played brilliantly as always and sobbed backstage and dried her eyes between pieces, then returned to the stage to resume her shining stage presence, again and again. To her audiences she was indefatigable; in her heart and soul, she was falling to pieces.

♥ Clara and Johannes: The Letters

Clara and Johannes likely exchanged hundreds, if not thousands, of letters over the course of their forty-year friendship, but very few survived because Brahms was so intent on destroying all his personal papers, either by burning them or tossing them into the Rhine. Bits and pieces that Clara hung on to illuminate just how all-encompassing their relationship was, from his declaration to her, while Robert was in the hospital and she was on tour—"I can do nothing but think of you and gaze constantly at your dear letter and portrait. What have you done to me? Can't you remove the spell you have cast over me?"—to her offer to manage his finances—"I wish you would give me your money to keep for you! Why do you always carry it about you?"

In the summer of 1856, Schumann started to truly slip away, just as his doctors had anticipated and as Clara and Johannes dreaded. For months he'd subsisted on nothing but consommé and wine. Finally Clara bucked his doctors and demanded a visit with her dying husband, on July 27. She hadn't seen him in over two years, and my heart broke when I read Robert's last words to her: "My Clara, I know you." He died two days later during the sliver of time that Clara and Johannes left his side to pick up another close friend at the train station.

Now, you'd think that this would have been the moment, tragic though it was, that they had been waiting for. Amid the devastation of their shared grief, the elephant in the living room was stomping its feet: Would Johannes marry the now-free Clara?

Sometime during a vacation in the Swiss Alps, this first chapter in their ongoing ambiguous relationship came to a close with what must have been a memorably challenging conversation. Johannes told Clara that no, after two years of pining for her, of shared anguish and joy in music, of maintaining a joint and excruciatingly long vigil regarding Robert's fate, and the suspended animation of being the de facto father to her children, he would not marry her.

Now, there could have been any number of reasons for his ultimate rejection of her, not the least of which was their age difference. Clara was by this time thirty-six and Brahms just twenty-three; even though she had proved herself as her family's breadwinner, social convention at the time would have required that Brahms step up to the plate to bring home the bacon if they married, and that could well torpedo his career. But there are also plenty of other, more intimate reasons that could explain why Brahms shied. His mother was seventeen years older than his father, and they had a fractious marriage, so he might have worried that that didn't bode well for his own union to an older woman. Then there's the possibility that if they did consummate the relationship, their coupling just wasn't to Brahms's taste—God knows it wouldn't be the first time a couple had had fantastic intellectual chemistry only to find disappointment between the sheets. But Swafford maintains that Brahms's adolescence working in brothels might well have scarred him for life. He had an appetite for prostitutes, and when push came to shove, maybe his early exposure to sordid situations had made him an emotional cripple insofar as transforming longing into fulfillment.

Whatever the case, the long and short of it was that within a few weeks of her beloved husband's dying, the bottom dropped out of the future Clara likely thought she had with Brahms. He left and went back to Hamburg. She wrote that her return from the train station, where she'd seen him off, was like coming home after a funeral.

Friends Without Benefits

Fortunately for Brahms, loyalty was a quality that Clara modeled as expertly as she did pride and fastidiousness. Rather than her kicking him to the curb for leading her on and then letting her down in her time of need, they entered into a new phase of their relationship—one in which they remained emotionally intimate and continued to collaborate musically, maintaining a robust if often querulous correspondence that often included veiled references to his rejection of her as well as bickering over, say, pedal points in his composition.

If they'd reached a resolution to the "unanswered question" that had hung over their heads for more than two years, that didn't mean that salt didn't still sting their wounds, as Brahms found out while on vacation with Clara and her family in 1858. Perhaps emboldened by his experience with Clara, Brahms got himself a girlfriend, the soprano Agathe von Siebold, but he misjudged and grabbed at her behind some bushes within eyeshot of Clara. As Swafford tells it, Clara stormed off, packed up her children, and left. (Brahms actually proposed to Agathe, and she agreed to marry him, but he dumped her before long, at which point one wonders if Clara saw the beginnings of a pattern.)

By around 1860, Brahms's career as a composer and conductor was slowly gathering steam. He had what one could call a grassroots following—he received occasional court appointments, and his concerts, while they were sometimes met with vigorous hissing, got press, plus he was composing at a furious rate. For a while, since an actual wife might tie down *l'artiste* too much, the attentions of singers, including vigorous flirtations with members of the *Frauenchor* (female choir singers) who performed his works, stroked his ego and kept him entertained. Meanwhile Clara, now in her forties and possibly on some level motivated by revenge, embarked on a super-secret affair with Brahms's friend and fellow composer Theodor Kirchner.

In 1868, Brahms premiered *Ein deutsches Requiem*—a massively complex choral and orchestral work that he'd been working on for over ten years, and his longest composition. It was likely infused to a certain degree with grief over his beloved mother's death just a few years earlier, and it marked a turning point in his career. On Good Friday 1868, it premiered at Bremen Cathedral— and Clara, to whom he'd recently been particularly obnoxious, yet again, made a last-minute trip to cheer him on. Once the audience had settled into their seats, Brahms took Clara's arm and walked her from the cathedral doors up the nave—a weddinglike procession of two, the significance of which would not have been lost on the crowd. That performance, with Brahms conducting, brought Clara to tears and marked the moment of Brahms's arrival as a key figure in the European musical scene.

Shock and Awe

But then, in May 1869, the moment that would have broken far sturdier relationships: Clara told Johannes that her twenty-four-year-old daughter Julie had received a proposal of marriage from an Italian count and had said "yes." Brahms ran from the house. In what must have been a tsunami wave of understanding, it became clear why Brahms had been such a terrific jerk for several years: He had fallen in love with her daughter. Suddenly it all added up: why the lovely Julie was awkward around him, why he was awkward around her, why he was so quick to snap at Clara.

To be fair, in many ways for Brahms a relationship with Julie would have been far more appropriate than one with her mother—a difference of twelve years between a man in his mid-thirties and a bride-to-be in her early twenties was more conventional then than not. Were it not for the fact that Johannes had essentially been her father figure for years—and that he might or might not have had an affair with her mother—Julie would have been a great, even a healthy choice in a mate for Brahms.

Perhaps Clara recognized this, and rather than fall into a rage—as many women would upon realizing that her daughter had replaced her in an intimate male friend's romantic attachment—she responded with compassion. And when Brahms threw himself into composing *Alto Rhapsody*, which he called a bridal song and gave as a wedding gift to Julie and her count, Clara wrote in her journal that the piece "seems to me neither more nor less than the expression of his own heart's anguish. If only he would for once speak as tenderly!"

The debacle with Julie ushered in a Pax Romana between Clara and Johannes that would, for the most part, last the rest of their lives as they saw each other through more good and bad times. As Clara aged, she became more and more tormented by injuries (although obviously her fingers were athletes, the rest of her was famously clumsy), and excruciating pain in her arms—probably from tendinitis or neuralgia—started to take its toll. To make matters worse, she began to lose her hearing around 1870, which caused new misery when she listened to orchestral works. And most tragically, death settled on her children like crows: Julie, who had been delicate for years, died at age twenty-seven of tuberculosis after giving birth to two children; Ludwig was declared incurably insane and was institutionalized; Felix, who was born shortly after Robert went mad and of whom Brahms once wrote, "I don't know how I should contain myself with happiness if I had a son like Felix," died of tuberculosis at age twenty-four; and

Ferdinand suffered from a morphine addiction and died at age forty-two. Only four of her eight children who survived infancy outlived her. Moreover, while she was a star into her sixties, in the last few decades her playing style had become a relic. The far more dramatic style of her rival Franz Liszt had triumphed in the court of public opinion. One person who saw one of her late performances remembered her as a "dumpy old lady in a cap"—a violent tumble from the peak of her celebrity.

♥ Rivals: Franz Liszt and Clara Schumann

Although she initially was impressed by Franz Liszt's music and performances, Clara Schumann came to hate him and his work with a passion. She was bitterly offended by his ostentatious interpretation of her husband, Robert's, work, and she likely took issue with his overt preference for life among the aristocracy. Liszt once published an article that wryly referred to her as a "stern priestess" and privately wrote to Marie d'Agoult that she was "a very simple person," but likely in public he was gracious to her, no doubt infuriating her all the more.

Meanwhile Johannes settled into a comfortable, lone-wolf bachelorhood, as detailed in Swafford's biography. He moved into a simple apartment, cluttered with books and papers and smelling of tobacco, and joined the landlady in the afternoon to chop vegetables. For his dinner he ate cold meat and sardines at home, slurping up the oil from the tin in the distinctly lower-class style of his roots. When he went on his daily walks, the bicyclists new to the streets drove him to distraction, but when street children swarmed around him, he passed out sweets to them. His trademark shabbiness made him even more reminiscent of a classic absentminded professor as he grew older—if his pants hung too far down over his walking boots . . . well then, he simply hacked them off with scissors. And as for his relationship with Clara, it remained as tortured as ever, Clara once confessing to a friend, "Would you believe that in spite of our intimate friendship Johannes has never told me anything about what excites or upsets him? He's just as much of a riddle, I could say almost as much of a stranger, as he was to me twenty-five years ago."

By the early 1890s, with Clara's health failing and Brahms now approaching sixty himself, he asked Clara to return all his letters. Having learned a lesson from Beethoven's death, when his private papers became public fodder, Brahms had always destroyed many of his personal documents, but now he made a mission of it. He pointed out that while Clara had children to protect her privacy after she died, he, like Beethoven, did not. When he returned her letters to him, for her to destroy, she read them and found them "one wail of sorrow," she wrote in her journal; she balked over handing over his to her and in the end appears to have handed over some, but not all, of them and kept copies, while Brahms made a project of guaranteeing that nothing was left. Confident that Clara would die before him, he reassured her that she and her husband "constitute the most beautiful experience of my life, and represent all that is rich and most noble in it."

During their last visit together, Clara played (no doubt with excruciating pain), his Six Pieces for Piano, op. 118, which he'd written and dedicated to her in 1893. Eugenie, her daughter, remembered later that when she heard the music stop, she joined them and saw that her seventy-six-year-old mother's cheeks were pink and her eyes glistening. Brahms sat across from Clara, also teary. "Your mother has been playing most beautifully for me," he said. He bade Eugenie to find a copy of a Beethoven sonata among Clara's scores, and he pointed out a mistake that Clara had found, and of course set right. "No other musician has an ear like that," Eugenie remembered he'd said.

In the spring of 1996, Clara had a stroke. Brahms wrote *Vier ernste Gesänge—Four Serious Songs*, which are in essence death chants—while he waited for word that she was near the end.

When she finally did pass on, miscommunications delayed Brahms, according to Swafford, and he arrived just after the funeral, during the procession to her grave next to Robert's. An onlooker remembered that rather than join the procession Brahms sobbed on the neck of a close friend behind some funeral wreaths. He said his last good-bye to the true love of his life by tossing three handfuls of dirt into her grave. He later said, "Now I have nothing left to lose." He followed his muse to the grave within a year.

♥ The Brahms Heartbreak Playlist

String Sextet no. 2 in G Major, op. 36

This incredibly intimate yet agitated piece is widely thought to express a heartbroken good-bye to Agathe von Siebold, the soprano to whom Brahms was briefly engaged. Hidden in its last climactic section are the notes AGADHE ADE, which several Brahms biographers are certain deliberately spell out "Farewell, Agathe."

A German Requiem, to Words of the Holy Scriptures, op. 45

This is Brahms's longest composition, clocking up to eighty minutes when performed. It's a choral piece, and only to his closest friends did Brahms admit that it is largely a meditation on the death of his long-suffering mother, a seamstress.

Alto Rhapsody, op. 53

Brahms wrote *Alto Rhapsody* as a wedding gift to Julie Schumann, with whom he himself was madly in love, and he called it his "bridal song."

Six Pieces for Piano, op. 118

Brahms wrote these works for Clara near the end of their lives, and they're comparatively short because Clara was in such pain that she could play for only brief periods of time.

Vier ernste Gesänge (Four Serious Songs)

Just after he heard that Clara had had a stroke, Brahms wrote *Four Serious Songs*. He publicly dedicated them to a friend whose father had recently died, but privately he would admit that he did write them for Clara. He could never bear to hear them sung in concert, and he cried when he himself played them.

The Alpha Cynic

IF YOU'RE FLIRTING with the notion that love might not *ever* be in the cards for you, then Morrissey is your man. As one of the greatest lyricists of frustrated desire, Morrissey sends the message (among many) that *love simply doesn't work for everyone*. Sometimes militantly asexual and cryptic about his history of celibacy, he is the quintessential pop-star paradox: He models his message by making himself the ultimate unattainable object. "I've always felt *above* sex. . . . Being only with yourself can be much more intense," he once said.

Anyone else coiffing their eccentricities and influences as relentlessly as Morrissey does would be fatiguing at best and laughable at worst, but Morrissey is, well . . . *Morrissey*. His arrogance and narcissism are, strangely, seductive and accessible. As detailed in *Mozipedia: The Encyclopedia of Morrissey and the Smiths*, his influences cover an impressive expanse (Feminism! Murder! The Beatles! Caligula! Joni Mitchell!), and how can one not be fascinated by so brilliant a man who has declared affection for such diverse creations as "Afternoon Delight," the 1976 hit paean to daytime sex; Dionne Warwick's "Loneliness Remembers What Happiness Forgets"; Brigitte Bardot's 1960s pop music; Chopin's nocturnes (how banal!); *Far from the Madding Crowd* specifically, but not

Thomas Hardy generally; the works of George Eliot and the Brontës; British TV soap operas such as *Coronation Street* (but only in its heyday); actress Bea Arthur of *Maude* and *Golden Girls* fame; *Cagney and Lacey*; bland food; stationery; swimming; and exceedingly weak tea.

Once asked when he was happiest, Morrissey said, "May 21, 1959"—that was the day before he was born. The impossibility of happiness, at least as the product of engagement with other people, is his mantra. One of his favorite actresses is reportedly the rebellious, withering, and famously cynical Hollywood legend Bette Davis, now deceased, who was married four times and finally came to the conclusion that work, not relationships, was the only lasting fulfillment to be had in life. It's easy to imagine him taking a cue from a classic Davis line in *All About Eve*: "Fasten your seat belts. It's going to be a bumpy night." For Morrissey and Davis, intellectual engagement rather than romantic love just might be the key to happiness. To those whom love seems to lead only to disappointment, Morrissey would likely advise getting your brain engaged and your intellect in gear.

Morrissey was the lyricist and front man for the Smiths from 1982 to 1987 and subsequently embarked on a stellar solo career. Check out these songs from different chapters of his life as cult icon extraordinaire:

"Asleep"
"Please, Please, Please, Let Me Get What I Want"
"Heaven Knows I'm Miserable Now"
"There Is a Light That Never Goes Out"
"The Boy with the Thorn in His Side"
"Last Night I Dreamt That Somebody Loved Me"
"Disappointed"
"Driving Your Girlfriend Home"
"The Edges Are No Longer Parallel"
"Girlfriend in a Coma"
"Half a Person"
"Happy Lovers at Last United"
"He Cried"
"Honey, You Know Where to Find Me"
"I Don't Mind If You Forget Me"
"I Want the One I Can't Have"
"I'm Not Sorry"
"I'm OK by Myself"
"Miserable Lie"
"The More You Ignore Me, the Closer I Get"
"Whatever Happens, I Love You"

Riddle in an Apricot Scarf

For decades now Carly Simon has yanked the world's chain over who stars in her 1970s hit "You're So Vain," which more than forty years after its release remains her signature song. Who is the narcissist with the Learjet, who swans into parties like a primo ballerino and spends his time with some version of James Bond?

In no particular order, the candidates for the song's inspiration include Mick Jagger (with whom Carly is rumored to have canoodled while she was engaged to James Taylor and who sings backup on the original recording—apparently much to Bianca Jagger's chagrin at the time), Warren Beatty (the most popular candidate, who in 2007 told an interviewer that the song was definitely about him), David Bowie, David Cassidy, Kris Kristofferson, and Cat Stevens. Simon has variously indicated that she'll reveal her muse in due time, that it's a composite of different men from her L.A. days, and that the one in the apricot scarf was Nick Nolte. It's a decades-old tease.

But speculation about the man in the song, tantalizing though it is, winds up eclipsing the song's real meaning, in which it makes no difference who exactly the man is and how extravagantly and publicly he polishes his ego. Even when the song came out and was reviewed by *Rolling Stone* in early 1973, I think its reviewer somewhat missed the point, calling it "an affectionately high-spirited putdown of a male chauvinist glamour boy." Set aside the glittering *who?* for a moment, as she implies with her suggestion that only he would think the song was *about him*, and it's about the reckoning, often with a hefty side of sour grapes, we undergo when a relationship has ended. It's about our quiet, introspective search—the clouds in our coffee—for an explanation of why it didn't work, and our eventual reassurances to ourselves that, really and truly, we are better off without him. For us mere mortals who don't bet on horses at Saratoga, jet from place to place in a Lear or walk into parties knowing we can have anyone there we want, the lessons are perhaps framed by more mundane circumstances, but they're equally important: *He didn't treat me well. He wasn't trustworthy. We didn't share the same values.*

Other songs about heartbreak performed by Carly Simon that have aged well:

"Haven't Got Time for the Pain"
"That's the Way I've Always Heard It Should Be"
"You Belong to Me"
"I've Got to Have You"

Two Heartbreak Classics:
"Suzanne" and "Hallelujah"

IN THE SONG "Pennyroyal Tea," off the album *In Utero*, Kurt Cobain sang, "Give me a Leonard Cohen afterworld / So I can sigh eternally." The year after the album was released, Cobain committed suicide, and one can only hope that his dream for an eternal sound track of Leonard Cohen came true.

For many music fans, songwriter Leonard Cohen (born in 1934) flies under the radar. If there are writers' writers, like Elizabeth Bishop or Denis Johnson or Vladimir Nabokov, then there must be songwriters' songwriters, in which case Leonard Cohen would reign supreme. As Lou Reed once said, Leonard Cohen belongs to the "highest and most influential echelon of songwriters." And then, among the many gorgeous songs he's written, two oft-covered love songs in particular stand out in the Zeitgeist for their impressionistic delicacy and wistfulness: "Suzanne" and "Hallelujah."

"Suzanne" can easily be interpreted as the story of a seduction, of one in which a man is drawn to a woman who is "half crazy" and plies him with tea and oranges, whom he wants to make love to but also take care of. In reality, though, it was inspired by a nonsexual relationship Cohen had in the summer of 1965 with a woman by the name of Suzanne Verdal, the then-wife of sculptor

Armand Vaillancourt. It is not so much about consummating a deeply felt emotional connection as it is about thinking about it and reflecting on the communion between two souls, each heartbroken in different ways. The song is, without a doubt, excruciatingly intimate.

For those who know Montreal, where Cohen and Verdal lived at the time, the lyrics are particularly resonant: The river is the St. Lawrence, and the honey-lit "lady of the harbor" alludes to the eighteenth-century Notre-Dame-de-Bon-Secours that sits on the port of Montreal, known as the Sailors' Church—a sweet link to the lines in the song about Jesus proclaiming that all men will live and die on the sea. As for Suzanne, she was the muse for Montreal's Beats in the 1960s, and during that summer of 1965 she spent much time with Cohen, drinking tea and eating oranges with him in her rustic apartment. She explained in a 1998 interview with the BBC that she was incredibly sad during that period over her recent split with Vaillancourt, with whom she had a daughter, but she was also, as she put it, on her own "creative drive." Verdal herself called what she and Cohen shared "a spirit union," adding that Cohen was "'drinking me in' more than I even recognized. . . . I took that time for granted. I would speak and I would move and I would encourage and he would just kind of like sit back and grin while soaking it all up and I wouldn't always get feedback, but I felt his presence really being with me. We'd walk down the street, for instance, and the click of our shoes, his boots and my shoes, would be like in synchronicity. . . . We'd almost hear each other thinking."

But much as "Suzanne" is about communion, I think it's ultimately more about emotional nudity, about the appeal, even the sexiness, of a grieving woman. In watching and fantasizing about a woman coping with heartbreak, Cohen is the voyeur.

"Suzanne" and Leonard Cohen rocketed to fame the next year,

when Judy Collins included the song on her 1966 album, *In My Life*—before Cohen even recorded an album himself. It's since been performed by Nina Simone, Roberta Flack, Harry Belafonte, Tori Amos, James Taylor, and Tangerine Dream; even Bruce Springsteen, it is said, performed the song early in his career when he fronted the Castiles. So subtle is the song's creep that when R.E.M. completed the song "Hope" in 1998, it was so similar to "Suzanne" in not just melody but lyrical structure, and even in its use of the second person, that they gave Cohen joint credit for it.

Imagine for a moment what it must have been like when Suzanne and Cohen saw each other in a hotel, as Suzanne said in her interview that they did, by which time it was clear his very sensual song about her was making him famous. It was, Suzanne recalled, a beautiful reunion, but one that ended oddly when, as she diplomatically puts it, "the moment arose that we could have a moment together intimately, and I declined." Whether it was that tension or a later one, for some reason that Suzanne herself said she didn't understand, they did not remain friends over the long term. When asked if she ever felt used, Suzanne responded that that is what poets do: create and move on; moreover, she said, the fact that she and Cohen are no longer close brings her some sadness. "Now the words have more meaning in a sense, because there's a kind of detachment in the song that I hear now, that I didn't hear then," she said.

Hallelujah

Then, if there's ever a song that has taken on a life of its own, even more than "Suzanne," it's Cohen's "Hallelujah," which has spawned at least a hundred recorded versions, the most famous ones by Jeff Buckley, John Cale, Rufus Wainwright (the *Shrek* version), 2008 *X Factor* winner Alexandra Burke, and k.d. lang. According to

Cohen's partner Anjani Thomas, in *Wears the Trousers* magazine, when the two of them heard lang's performance of his masterwork back in 2006, they looked at each other and said, "Well, I think we can lay that song to rest now. It's really been done to its ultimate blissful state of perfection." But given that it's been used ad nauseam in sound tracks for TV series such as *The O.C.*, *The West Wing*, *ER*, and *Scrubs*, it's fair to say, as Cohen himself has even admitted, that primal and sublime as the song is, it has marched into the realm of cliché. "I think it's a good song," Cohen told the CBC in 2009, "but I think too many people sing it." That said, Cohen is surely wincing his way all the way to the bank: He made millions in royalties off Alexandra Burke's version alone.

♥ Hallelujah Chutzpah

"Hallelujah" was first released on Cohen's album *Various Positions*, and he apparently once told Bob Dylan, who has performed it live, that it took him two years to write. It's been performed by almost two hundred artists in various languages, including in Italian by the pop-operatic boy band Il Divo, and the Israeli Defense Force reportedly broadcasts what one assumes is a Hebrew version every Saturday at 2:00 AM on its radio channel; so deeply engrained is "Hallelujah" in the international Zeitgeist that an entire BBC radio documentary was devoted to it. Sheryl Crow, Susan Boyle, Regina Spektor, and Jon Bon Jovi have all pulled off respectable versions, but when Justin Timberlake and Matt Morris took it on for Hope for Haiti Now in 2011, the result was an epic failure. Equal injustice was done to it by Avril Lavigne.

But putting aside the fact that it has become a cliché, it's easy to get so distracted by the beauty of the melody and the transcendent chorus that one doesn't even attempt to figure out what it means. On one hand, "Hallelujah" is of course spiritual, and on the other it is, or can be when issued from the vocal cords of the right person, incredibly sexy, making it about the spirituality of sex. Jeff Buckley called it a "hallelujah to the orgasm," and British singer Kathryn Williams once prepped her audience for her version of it with the statement, "I really, really, really want to shag Leonard Cohen." According to the British *Telegraph* article "20 Facts About Leonard Cohen's Hallelujah," Cohen himself said that the song "explains that many kinds of hallelujahs do exist, and all the perfect and broken hallelujahs have equal value."

Perhaps, then, heartbreak counts as well among the hallelujahs: We should cherish and even celebrate disappointments in love, including the mourning itself, to the point of near religious respect.

The Call of Duende

PUNK FANS RESPOND to the fire and brimstone of Nick Cave and his persona—one can imagine him as a whip-bearing minister, living alone in a Gothic castle, clad in his trademark black. But read—or better yet, listen to—the love-song lecture that he delivered in Vienna in 1999 (*The Secret Life of the Love Song*) and one is astonished by the tenderness, as well as by the astounding beauty, of his writing.

For those not familiar with Cave's background, it's important to know that his father, an English teacher, died in a car crash when Cave was nineteen; at the moment Nick was informed of the tragedy, his mother was bailing him out of jail for burglary. "The loss of my father created in my life a vacuum, a space in which my words began to float and collect and find their purpose," he told a reporter for the British newspaper *The Independent* in 2008. For Cave, creativity depends on loss, and even sorrow itself is a creative act.

It makes sense, then, that Cave is a master of sad love songs and that he is fascinated by duende—a tough-to-translate term popularized by the Spanish writer Federico García Lorca that roughly means "the power of dark emotion." All truly successful love songs, Cave suggests in his lecture, are vessels for duende. "Those songs that speak of love without having within their lines an ache or a sigh are not love songs . . . and are not to be trusted," he argues, following up with the spectacular line, "The love song must resonate with the susurration of sorrow, the tintinnabulation of grief." (To spare you having to look these words up, as I did once I got over reveling in their beauty, "susurration" means "a whispering sound or a murmur," and "tintinnabulation" means "the sounding of bells." Another wonderful term Cave introduces in the lecture is "erotographomania"—the obsessive writing of love letters.) Most of today's pop music, he maintains, slams a door in the face of authentic sorrow—all it does is "hurl dollops of warm, custard-colored baby vomit down the airwaves."

He goes on to explain that his song "Far from Me," on the album *The Boatman's Call*, chronicles, from start to finish, a four-month-long relationship. "Far from Me" was written more or less in real time—a verse per month as the relationship budded, bloomed, withered and died, and it captures the whole cycle from innocence and the unawareness that "at any day the bottom would drop out of the whole thing" to the end, when the song could only be completed upon catastrophic ending of the romance. "I find quite often that the songs I write seem to know more about what is going on in my life than I do," he said. And in "Far from Me," he was able to transform a relationship into a song, and with the song he has the more enduring, spiritual connection. "The relationship . . . has been and gone, but the song itself lives on, keeping a pulse running through my past."

The lecture is packed with gorgeous metaphors, but for me among the most beautiful is the notion that his songs are his "crooked brood of sad-eyed children" who surround, protect, and comfort him. Artists often think of their work as their children. They are, after all, products of love and, with that, products of heartbreak as well.

Mix Tapes

NEVER IN MY life have I grieved the loss of what was essentially a pile of plastic more than I did when someone broke into my Mazda and stole an entire bag of my emotional history: my tape collection. Some stranger was huffing down the dark streets with a paper bag stuffed chock-full of *me*. Worth nothing to anyone else in the world, that brown bag had sat in the well of the right rear seat for years, and I'd reach back while driving, plunge my hand elbow-deep into the bag, and grab whatever had gotten squished at the bottom. I was my own deejay day after day, commute after commute, and even during the time I drove across the country alone (in December, no less). Phil Collins's *Face Value*, the sound track to the very first time I ever really truly made out with a guy; the little-known first Supertramp album, which my brother and I obsessed over and which I still insist is supremely brilliant; *Hot Rocks*, *The Joan Baez Lovesong Album*, Joe Jackson's *Beat Crazy*, Talking Heads' *Little Creatures*, Marti Jones's *Unsophisticated Time* and *Any Kind of Lie*, the sound track to the Wim Wenders film *Until the End of the World*, and so many more—gone, in an instant. With the exception of the Joan Baez, which appears to have faded into the ether of obscure seventies compilations that no one gives a shit about and reissued on CD, these albums were in theory replaceable.

What was not replaceable were the many mix tapes in that bag—ones I'd made myself to capture a summer or an afternoon and ones friends had made for me that were filled with songs I didn't have in my own collection, where Pat Metheny bunked with Jethro Tull and Siouxsie and the Banshees and that version of "Ave Maria" by the West India Company that I can only describe as Hindustani disco. Into thin air went "Chin Up, Little Buckeroo," a mix a friend sent once when I was dumped, featuring lots of Lyle Lovett, that did in fact make me chin up. Gone were mixes from people I'd long since lost touch with. Gone as well were the mixes of coy courtship—the few in my collection that some earnest boy had taken such care in creating.

Which brings us to the care. In the 2000 film *High Fidelity*, the main character, a record-store owner, offers instructions on the subtle art of making a truly unshakable mix that still respects the fact that you are tinkering with other people's poetry, manipulating it to convey just how you feel. "Now, the making of a great compilation tape, like breaking up, is hard to do and takes ages longer than it might seem," he says. "You gotta kick off with a killer, to grab attention. Then you got to take it up a notch, but you don't wanna blow your wad, so then you got to cool it off a notch." And, he points out in the very last lines of the movie, it's important that you construct a mix tape for a loved one out of music that that person will like, rather than what you think she should like. Constructing a mix tape that celebrates someone else's taste rather than imposing your own is part of the trick.

Looking back on it, I think mix tapes were a way of saying, "Our relationship might not last forever, but you will always remember me every time you hear these songs." There was an alluring paradox to this, though, given the mix tape's very delicacy, its vulnerability to a hot dashboard or old man winter, and the specter that any moment it could break and maddeningly unfurl—if it crumpled in the unfurling, then no amount of winding it back with a pencil could repair it. Maybe mix tapes were not just sound tracks to phases in our lives, they were themselves metaphors for love.

In the iTunes world, burning playlists onto CDs for your loved ones of course has its advantages, like being able to keep a copy for yourself and the ability to easily replace the original if your friend loses it, but I think the permanence of the playlist and the ease with which a mix can be re-created undermines the message—or at least what *was* the message with a good ol' mix tape. Love's labor is lost.

Suggested Sound Tracks

Here are some of my favorite songs for various stages of a breakup that, in my opinion, can significantly invigorate the heartbreak experience.

Watching-It-All-Fall-Apart Mix:

- "The Last Day of Our Acquaintance," Sinéad O'Connor
- "Love Will Tear Us Apart," Joy Division
- "I Love You, But Goodbye," Langhorne Slim
- "Make This Go On Forever," Snow Patrol
- "The Leaving Song," Chris Garneau
- "The End Has Begun," Loudon Wainwright III

Just-Want-to-Wallow Mix:

- "Good Morning, Heartache," Billie Holiday
- "I'm So Lonesome I Could Cry," Hank Williams

- "Why Does My Heart Feel So Bad?" Moby
- "Cosmic Love," Florence + the Machine
- "I Wish I Never Saw the Sunshine," Beth Orton
- "I'm Nobody's Baby," Judy Garland

I-Can't-Stand-the-Thought-of-You Mix:

- "You Oughta Know," Alanis Morissette
- "Before He Cheats," Carrie Underwood
- "Miserable Lie," the Smiths
- "My Sweet Fracture," Saves the Day
- "Go to Hell," Nina Simone
- "Lover I Don't Have to Love," Bright Eyes

. . . But-I-Wish-You-Were-Here Mix:

- "How Can You Mend a Broken Heart?" Al Green
- "I'm a Fool to Want You," Frank Sinatra
- "He Stopped Loving Her Today," George Jones
- "Without You," Harry Nilsson
- "I Fall to Pieces," Patsy Cline
- "I'm Not Missing You," Bering Strait

Psych-Up Mix (best played loud in the car):

- "Feeling Good," Nina Simone/Muse
- "I've Forgotten What It Was in You (That Put the Need in Me)," Maria McKee
- "I Will Survive," Gloria Gaynor, also performed by Cake
- "Wish Me Well (You Can Go to Hell)," the Bouncing Souls
- "Over You," Roxy Music
- "Killin' Kind," Shelby Lynne

It's-Over-But-I-Still-Think-About-You Mix:

- "You Could Be Happy," Snow Patrol
- "Keep Me in Your Heart," Warren Zevon
- "Martha," Tom Waits
- "Missing," Everything but the Girl
- "I Will Not Forget You," Sarah McLachlan
- "Lover, You Should've Come Over," Jeff Buckley

Art

Roy Lichtenstein's 1964 painting *Ohhh...Alright...* depicts a young redhead clutching a phone, her brow furrowed, lips pursed, and looking utterly vulnerable and crestfallen. While of course any work of art is open to interpretation, it's clear that this painting captures a moment in a larger narrative, and my guess is that she's fallen head over heels for a guy who's just for the first time canceled a date. To me the painting pinpoints the moment it all turns south, the pinprick precursor to the broken heart: the broken plan. Lichtenstein painted *Ohhh...Alright...* and its sister paintings, all depicting comic-book women in states of duress just as his marriage was falling apart. *Ohhh...Alright...* sold in 2010 for $42.6 million.

This is a perfect example of a visual artist who channeled his personal heartbreak into his art, but it also illustrates just how much our culture values the intersection between art and love gone wrong. As with music, knowing the backstory is a double-edged sword. If we choose to ignore the context of the creator's life, then we're free to embellish the work with our own experiences, but then again, knowing details about the artist's personal anguish can really make subject, color, and composition pop. Even with images that are not necessarily the product of one artist, like the graphic heart, drilling down into their origins changes our perceptions of them forever—just as heartbreak does to love.

Tracking the Graphic Heart

TRACKING THE ORIGIN of the graphic heart (♥) turned me into a Goldilocks of antecedents: One source was too religious, another too medical, another too simple, still another too New Agey. Whether we type it as an emoticon in a text message or proclaim I ♥ POMERANIANS! on our bumpers, the ♥ is one of the most stubborn and ubiquitous bits of shorthand to grace our daily lives, and more than a few noble souls have attempted to trace its origins. But the fact is that the ♥'s history is a tangle, and in it, associations between completely disparate traditions melded together, often losing their nativity in the process.

Blame It on Botany

The association between the ♥ and love—or love's compatriot, sex—likely first entered our visual lexicon through stylized depictions of plants—one ordinary, the other quite extraordinary.

Let's start with ivy, the ordinary. Along with attenuated and buff athletes, taut archers, and rearing stallions, heart-shaped ivy leaves were common decorations on ancient (and specifically Greek) vessels and amphorae. Vines in turn were associated with the party boy Dionysus, god of wine and ecstasy, who was also associated with sex—a well-founded case of guilt by association if there ever was one. And much as the Greeks tried to assign love and sex to separate stalls (see p. 59 for more on that), inevitably the two commingle, no matter what the cultural prohibitions are. So, by this genesis, the ♥'s early path in Western antiquity goes something like this: ivy leaf = vine leaf = wine = party = sex = love. Add in ivy's tenacity (ask any gardener—it's next to impossible to eradicate, and, left unchecked, it can destroy just about anything in its path), coupled with its tendency to "embrace," and you have an apt metaphor for enduring if pesky love.

But far more intriguing to me is the second botanical candidate: a plant called silphium.

Let's start our silphium exploration with a little time travel to the fifth century BC. Imagine for a moment that you're a Greek merchant living in a colony called Cyrene, on the North African coast of the Mediterranean (in present-day Libya). Container after container of *laserpicium*—that's silphium's sap or resin—has sailed on your boats to ports all over the Mediterranean. The plant is so important to the economy that the very coins that jingle in your purse are pressed with images of the plant's ridged stalk and feathery fronds and, more important to our story, a form that to the modern eye is distinctly heart-shaped.

What's so special about silphium? Sure, it fattens livestock, its flowers scent perfume, and chopped up it can season breakfast, lunch, and dinner, but it's also a known cure for a host of maladies—coughs and colds, nausea and indigestion, seizures, balding, leprosy, warts, edema, chilblains . . . and unwanted pregnancies. Better still, it's possible that it was believed to be the best deal in the history of pharmacology, a contraceptive *and* an aphrodisiac all in one.

The silphium plant was a member of the parsley family, many species of which are packed with estrogen. For ancient women around the Mediterranean, fending off the pitter-patter of unwelcome little feet depended on either brewing a tea from silphium leaves or mixing a pea-size ball of the resin in wine or inserting it as a suppository.

Pliny, the Roman naturalist who lived in the first century AD, called silphium "one of the most precious gifts from nature to man," but by his time it was nearly wiped out. By the end of the first century, thanks to energetic consumption and, possibly, the desertification of its native habitat, silphium was apparently gone.

But not before its association with sexuality became firmly entrenched. Witness one ancient Greek story in which two mythic hotties, Castor and Pollux—coincidentally on their way back from Cyrene—ask to spend a few nights in a Spartan's house. The man declines because his maiden daughter is home; he suggests they stay elsewhere. Come morning, his daughter and "all her girlish apparel" are gone, although she leaves behind statues of Castor and Pollux and some silphium. The modern equivalent? Robert Pattinson and Taylor Lautner, fresh from a trip to Bangkok, ask to crash at your place for the night, but, knowing your daughter's taste for the vampy boy toys, you suggest they move along. In the morning you find that your daughter has bolted with her entire wardrobe yet left behind her *Twilight* posters as well as her birth control.

But back to the heart shape on Cyrenean coins, which can be read in two different ways when it comes to the ♥ we know and love. One possibility is that the image is a stylized depiction of testicles, which among the ancients was definitely a visual shorthand for hot sex. In that case, then, the coin was basically an advertisement along the lines of a modern Budweiser commercial: "Buy Cyrenean silphium and get laid." The other possibility is that the heart shape depicts silphium's seed pod, a theory that got a boost around 1990 when a Bedouin guide led a team of archaeologists to a remote site where an unfamiliar plant that looked like ancient renditions of silphium grew, and sure enough its seed pods were heart-shaped. Either way, the shape was associated with sex.

Whether it was ivy or silphium or their combined efforts that form the basis of the ♥ as shorthand for sex we'll never know, but the Romans inherited the association. In one explicit, and indeed quite funny, discovery from the ruins of Ephesus, a once-Greek city that the Romans controlled in what is now Turkey, archaeologists painstakingly excavated ruins of a brothel from the first century AD. One of the first known examples of modern-style graffiti marks the way to the den of ill repute: A cluster of images in the marble paving include a heart shape, an X, the outline of a foot, some money, and a woman's head—the gist of which is "Turn left at the crossroads for booty." Hey, one has to give the artist credit for discreetly choosing a female head for his message; a lesser man would surely have represented another body part.

Enter Anatomy

But ivy and silphium, the allures of Castor and Pollux, and primitive advertisements scratched into a slab of marble don't explain our association between the heart icon, love, and the physical heart. For that we turn to Aristotle and the interpretations of his work that were the basis of medicine for centuries.

Aristotle (384–322 BC) was a man of many obsessions, among them anatomy. Although he likely never dissected a human cadaver, he maintained from his inspections of dead animals that the human heart contained three "cavities" (as opposed to four, as we now know), that it had a pointed end, and that it was the origin of life and the seat of emotions.

Now, this wasn't the very first time that the human heart had been linked with emotion—the ancient Egyptians made a connection between the physical heart and love, illustrated by the hiero-glyph *ib,* which is roughly heart-shaped and connotes "heart soul" in a physical as well as a sexual way. But in the medieval period, when scholars showed renewed interest in classical texts, some art-ists attempted to render Aristotle's textual description of a three-chambered heart with images that they thought more or less matched: large swells on each side representing two chambers and a dip in between them indicating a third, smaller chamber hidden behind. So those early renditions of what we would now call a heart shape, at least the ones that connote spirituality, are in part the result of the work of scribes who struggled with bungled trans-lations and had no knowledge of anatomy, plus that of the artists who were just as foiled.

But another graphic version of the human heart was floating around at more or less the same time—what's called the pinecone-shaped heart, also rooted in classical descriptions noting that the heart was shaped like a pinecone or an upside-down pyramid. It gets fuzzy here, but from what I can tell, by the time anatomists could confirm from dissections what a human heart—at least a dead human heart, that is—looked like once and for all, both the scalloped heart and the pinecone-shaped heart were common, de-pending on who was doing the drawing and in what context.

But by the thirteenth century or so, the scalloped heart—the one that most of us are most familiar with now—was deeply en-trenched. Its ascension during that particular period likely had everything to do with concurrent curiosity and ignorance about human anatomy, the advent of courtly love (if it existed), and burgeoning literacy and the production and circulation of illustrated books.

The Injured Heart—Stabbed, Sliced, and Diced

But as we all well know, the graphic heart isn't always an inviting, symmetrical whole—as often as not, it's shot through with arrows, pierced with daggers, or shattered like glass. If you take a close look at a remarkable German woodcut from around 1485 called *Venus and Her Lover*, a man kneels at the feet of a scantily clad Venus, both of them surrounded by no fewer than eighteen hearts in various states of duress: burned on a pyre, severed with a hacksaw, stabbed through with a sword, flattened in a vise, impaled on a lance, squashed in something that looks remarkably like a panini grill embellished with nails, and tormented by various and sundry other devices that are clearly the provenance of a well-equipped dungeon master. Needless to say, the message is clear: Mess with romantic love and pain is what awaits you.

This particular image riffs on Christian images of Jesus's wounds, including those to his heart, which were symbolic access points to his love. His wounds suggested a pathway, as if you could get away from it all by climbing inside Jesus for shelter. During the medieval period, Christ's wounds were the focus in the visual arts, but then over time his heart became ascendant, often stabbed by thorns, levitating over saints, pierced with a cross, spewing flames, or dripping blood. By the seventeenth century, obsession with the Sacred Heart of Jesus (typically rendered as gorily as possible) was a widespread cultural phenomenon, particularly in France. As Protestantism spread across Europe, for Catholics the injured heart, dripping blood, may well have signaled where they stood regarding transubstantiation, one of the hottest points of debate during the Reformation: Protestant thought maintains that the wine and the wafer ingested at the Eucharist are merely symbolic, while Catholics believe that they actually become the blood and the body of Christ. Blood aside, it could as well be that while Catholics were comfortable with elaborate depictions of Jesus's heart because it was in keeping with the elaborateness of Catholic practices overall, Protestants, with their emphasis on simplicity and rejection of icons, were perhaps more comfortable with the more subdued, discreet ♥.

Across the Atlantic, roughly around the same time, the Christian injured-heart tradition met its match in what is now Mexico. As Spanish colonists flooded the region, they took with them gory depictions of Jesus's heart, which promptly collided with the natives' own bloody traditions, like animal sacrifice (Mayan) and human sacrifice (Aztec), as well as a cultural zeal for hearts. One couldn't ask for a more perfect union in terms of diverse religious traditions sharing fundamentals: The Aztecs maintained that their sun god drank the human blood spilled during sacrifice, and Christians drank the blood of their god during the Eucharist. Then, as more and more natives became Catholic, the stage was set for a virtual riot of bloody Christian hearts in Mexican religious art. Centuries after the native and Spanish colonial traditions of bloody hearts merged, the half-Catholic Mexican artist Frida Kahlo captured the cultural, religious, and artistic convergence of the traditions to fabulous effect in one of her most famous paintings. *Two Fridas* features two self-portraits, each marked by its own external and anatomically correct heart—one healthy, one dripping blood—a far-from-oblique reference to the heartbreak she suffered thanks to her philandering husband, Diego Rivera.

No matter what the context, religious or romantic, perhaps images of injured hearts are all about what we might call "flow"—the movement and exchange between exterior and inner experience, from the past and present into the future, and from the temporal to the ecstatic. Looked at from this perspective, a wounded heart isn't all bad. It implies the possibility of transformation.

In *The Book of the Heart*, Louisa Young notes that the Olmecs, predecessors to the Mayans and the Aztecs, are responsible for the oldest known three-dimensional, more or less anatomically correct representation of a human heart: a ceramic jar shaped like a heart but with the head of a man. His belly is rendered by two chambers and his arms embrace the three major blood vessels, with the aorta, the pulmonary artery, and the superior vena cava all readily discernible. It's perfectly possible that four thousand years ago the vessel contained blood or hearts harvested in sacrifices. But truly accurate visuals of the human heart were still a long, long way away—the first anatomically accurate drawing of the human heart was by Leonardo da Vinci.

A Penny for Your Love

The religious history of the ♥ still doesn't explain why it became so entrenched to the point of cliché. For that we probably have the rise of paper valentines to thank. In the eighteenth century in England, just when the value of romantic love was being reassessed, penny posts allowed anyone to locally send an item (such as a valentine) cheaply, and in the early nineteenth century paper valentines were in such high demand that they were mass-produced in factories. Then, after England adopted the Uniform Penny Post (meaning that one could send an item anywhere in the United Kingdom with a prepaid stamp) in 1840, Valentine's Day took off like wildfire. According to some estimates, in the United States alone, each February 14 a billion valentines are exchanged, and that's not even counting the 15 million or so e-valentines that have gained popularity in the last decade, not to mention candy hearts or heart-shaped boxes of chocolate. Needless to say, the history of valentines alone accounts for a heck of a lot of ♥s floating around, absorbing into the Zeitgeist.

Then again, maybe the ♥'s popularity is due to influences far less material. There's a neat symmetry to the fact that just as anyone can love, anyone with a stick and a patch of dirt can draw a ♥. But ultimately I think the enduring nature of the ♥ has a lot to do with the terrifying subtext of the cleaving at the top: the suggestion of a weak point, and that it can break in two.

Edvard Munch (1863–1944)

WHEN I STARTED to study art and heartbreak, I asked a friend who was in the midst of a terrible, complicated split from her husband what works of art illustrated her state of mind. "Munch, *The Scream*, at least that's how I feel," she wrote back immediately.

In Norwegian, Munch's native language, *The Scream* series is called *Skrik*, which, since it's a cognate of "shriek," might mean that a better translation would be *The Shriek*.

She was referring to one of the most iconic images in the visual arts: Edvard Munch's *The Scream* series, which he started in 1893. In it a cadaverous, sexless figure (okay, so it looks a bit like a horror-struck alien), hands clapped to ears, emits a primal scream from a cavernous mouth against a background of sky layered with red and orange and swirls of blue water. Munch made numerous versions of it in various media, but the most famous one is a combination of oil, pastel, and tempera. According to the Art Institute of Chicago, which owns the lithograph version, *The Scream* was rooted in an experience he'd had in Oslo that he recorded in his diary:

> One evening I was walking along a path, the city was on one side and the fjord below. I felt tired and ill. I stopped and looked out over the fjord—the sun was setting, and the clouds turning blood red. I sensed a scream passing through nature; it seemed to me that I heard the scream. I painted this picture, painted the clouds as actual blood. The color shrieked.

There's something to my friend's association of the painting with the alienation, horror, and existential loneliness of heartbreak. Munch himself was fascinated and confounded by women, and art historians who specialize in Munch tend to agree that at its most fundamental his art was an attempt to exorcise his love demons. Even as a young man, he wrote, "Women are beautiful creatures, by the way. I think I shall paint only women from now on."

On some level *The Scream* might have been informed by an initiation and a heartbreak he'd suffered years earlier in Antwerp, when he was in his early twenties and had an affair with an older married woman whom he referred to in his notebooks as "Mrs. Heiberg" but in fact was a distant cousin's wife named Millie Thaulow. Their affair lasted for two years, often transpiring in the woods near a lovely fishing village called Aasgaardstrand. Of the affair with Millie, he later wrote, that "an experienced worldly woman came along and I got a baptism of fire—I had the misfortune to suffer passionate love . . . and for several years I was close to insanity."

But the truth is that Munch grappled with insanity and alcoholism for much of his life, both perhaps driven in part by his determination to maintain art above love—far above—in the pecking order of his priorities. This was a decision that caused him much guilt, particularly in his choice of art over one Tulla Larsen.

Munch and Tulla first met in 1898 when she visited his studio with a mutual friend, and from there they had an on-again, off-again relationship all over Europe, while he drifted in and out of sanatoriums and ramped up his drinking habit. Tulla was thirty-ish, unmarried, rich, and single-minded: She wanted Munch if it meant stalking him, even if he still declined to marry her when she gave him an antique wedding chest as a hint-hint gift. Only once he ran away from her in France when she thought they were there to get married did she seemingly give up.

The backdrop to Munch's second-best-known painting, *The Dance of Life*, depicts a party scene during a summer night in Aasgaardstrand and is widely thought to be influenced by Tulla's presence in Munch's life. Likely, as he and Tulla were in the midst of the throes of another where-do-we-go-from-here squabble around 1900, Munch painted *The Dance of Life*. While happy couples swirl and dance in the background, in the foreground on the left a woman in white looks happy and hopeful; in the middle a couple hold hands and dance stiffly, avoiding each other's gaze, the woman looking corpselike; and on the right a gaunt and haggard woman in black observes the scene. On the one hand, it could represent an expression of Munch's inability to have successful relationships, and on the other it's an explicit reference to his experiences with Millie and Tulla (his "dance" with Millie is in the center, flanked by disparate images of Tulla—one gentle and demure in white, the other in black, dark and desolate with disappointment). But levitating above these interpretations of the three figures, I think, is a meditation on the stages of romantic love, at least for people like Munch with complex heads and hearts. Stage 1: happiness and expectation. Stage 2: wrangling, trying to figure out how to move together as a couple. Stage 3: despair and alienation. Love and joy were something for other people, like the lusty dancers in the backdrop that Munch referred to as representing the "deranged dance of life." Happy love was not for Munch's ilk.

Perhaps with *Dance of Life*, thirty-seven-year-old Munch thought that he had exorcised his love demons once and for all. But no: When he retreated to his cottage in Aasgaardstrand in the summer of 1902, he took to more drinking and even public brawls. And then, after more than a year of his being Tulla-free, she returned. At first he refused to engage with her, but he relented when her friends told him that she was suicidal and dosing herself with hefty amounts of morphine. He should have stuck with his gut. When he finally went to see her, she was reportedly lying on her bed like a corpse, with candles near her head. Somehow her dramatic repose evolved into a scuffle between the two, with a revolver, although whose it was and who pulled the trigger has never been confirmed. At least one shot was fired, injuring Edvard, and rather than tend to his wounds, Tulla paced and then began mopping up the blood with a cloth.

After this violent final break with Tulla Larsen, Munch continued to reference their relationship in his paintings for at least another six years. In *Self-Portrait with Tulla Larsen* (1905), he painted them—both looking downright tubercular—on one canvas and then cleaved it in half to make it into two portraits; in *The Murderess* (1906), a man with a bloodied shirt lies prostrate on a bed while a Tulla-esque woman faces the viewer; and in *Death of Marat I* (1907), a man lies naked on a bloodied bed while yet another Tulla-esque, this time naked, woman faces the viewer.

Due to the struggle, Munch lost the middle finger on his left hand at the last knuckle. While the injury didn't affect his painting, it did embarrass and enrage him. For the rest of his days, he hid his injury from the world, always covering it in photographs and self-portraits, and when he died, forty pairs of gloves were found in his house. Surely every glance at his half-mast middle finger reminded him of how marked he was by love gone wrong. In contrast, Tulla moved on unblemished. Not too long after the incident, she married another artist, one of Munch's colleagues. Munch reflected later, as quoted in the *Smithsonian* magazine article "Edvard Munch: Beyond the Scream," "I had sacrificed myself needlessly for a whore." He continued to drink heavily and suffered occasional bouts of insanity from 1908 onward. He died at age eighty after years of semiseclusion, locked up with over twenty thousand pieces of his own work, which he regarded as his "children."

If his works were Munch's progeny, then they've done very well for themselves, particularly the four versions of *The Scream*. In May 2012, a pastel-on-board version of his depiction of the shriek of nature sold at auction to an anonymous bidder for a whopping $120 million.

Oskar Kokoschka

Of all the people I cover in this book, the Austrian expressionist painter Oskar Kokoschka (1886–1980) is the one with whom I wish I could have had a drink. Eccentricity in artists is of course nothing new, but his version, marinated as it was in spectacular obsession, really takes the cake.

Kokoschka's life has been called "one of the most extraordinary in the history of twentieth century art." He was born in a small town in Austria and first made his name painting portraits of Vienna's celebrity figures. He was found guilty of insubordination after he joined the army in 1914 and volunteered to go to the Eastern Front (not a pleasant place to be) in order to avoid imprisonment. While fighting, he took a bullet in his head and a bayonet in his lung. During World War II, his work was included by the Nazis under the rubric "degenerate art," and he fled first to Prague and then to the United Kingdom, but he ultimately settled in Switzerland and died at the ripe age of 93. Among his friends he was known as "OK" or "crazy Kokoschka." One friend recalled that he was a raconteur of "almost Homeric long-distance energy."[6]

But in addition to his artistic brilliance, his quirky generosity,

6 As quoted in the retrospective catalog of his work, *Oskar Kokoschka: 1886–1980.* London: Tate Gallery Publications, 1986.

and his storytelling abilities, Kokoschka was known for his obsession as a young man with one of the great femmes fatales of the early twentieth century: Alma Mahler.

In 1912, when twenty-six-year-old Oskar met thirty-three-year-old Alma, he was known as the bad boy of Vienna's art scene and she was known as the saucy socialite and widow of composer Gustav Mahler—if Vienna's newspapers of that time had had blind items, Alma and Oskar's liaison would surely have made the cut. Alma's stepfather had commissioned Oskar to paint a portrait of Alma, and before you could say "Please pass the turpentine," the artist and his muse started to get to know each other very intimately off canvas. It was a passionate affair: When Oskar wasn't having sex with Alma, he was painting her, and when he wasn't with her, he was writing letters to her. Over the course of their steamy but stormy three years as an item, he wrote her nearly four hundred letters, some of which are noble, some of which are obsessive, and many of which complain that she hasn't written him back. Consider this ultimatum from a July 1914 letter, published many years later by his wife of all people: "My darling Almi, You know you can wheedle everything you want out of me. Make up your mind to a proper life with me, and come to a decision about what will give you greater joy: me, you or other people." Right around the same time, the outbreak of World War I, for Alma it was all wearing thin.

> Kokoschka painted and drew Alma Mahler hundreds of times, but the most famous of these images is 1914's *Bride of the Wind (The Tempest)*, which he painted two years into their three-year affair. In it they're lying down together, half naked, she with her cheek on his shoulder asleep, he with his arm around her, awake and protective. Early that year Alma had gotten pregnant but had an abortion at a Viennese clinic, much to Kokoschka's distress.

Oskar spent the early winter of 1915 training as a cavalry officer, and Alma spent it deciding what to do with him. By April she'd reached her decision: Dump Oskar and marry the architect Walter Gropius, with whom she'd had an affair while married to her now-deceased husband. Months after their breakup, Kokoschka still wrote her letters of repudiation, noting her scorn, accusing her of never understanding him, threatening suicide, and saying passive aggressive things like "Don't be anxious on my account . . . my greatest concern is not knowing how things are with you. That's all that remains of the riches I had when I was beginning to love you: a beggar's mite."

Puppet Therapy

By the summer of 1918, still several months before the armistice that ended World War I, Oskar had recovered from his war wounds but not from Alma. So he took drastic therapeutic means: He ordered a life-size doll, to be in every detail the image of Alma, from a puppet maker in Munich named Hermine Moos. According to Alfred Weindinger's book *Kokoschka and Alma Mahler*, for six months Oskar fussed over the minutiae of his doll, modeling the head himself and sending it along, penning long letters to Hermine with directions ("Please make it possible that my sense of touch will be able to take pleasure in those parts where the layers of fat and muscle suddenly give way to a sinuous covering of skin"), as well as drafting life-size oil sketches—based on "actual measurements"—to inform the creation of Frau Mahler: The Doll. In anticipation he ordered the best Parisian clothes for the doll, just as Alma wore.

Sexual attraction to statues, dolls, and mannequins (and presumably puppets!) is called agalmatophilia, and it's nothing new. In Ovid's *Metamorphoses*, Pygmalion falls in love with his own sculpture of a woman: "His kisses / He fancies, she returns; he speaks to her, / Holds her, believes his fingers almost leave / An imprint on her limbs. . . ." As he stroked her, her body "softened like wax in sunshine."

When the completed doll moved in with him to his apartment in Dresden in February 1919, Oskar's elderly butler had a stroke as it (she?) was unpacked, so thrilling was the event. According to translations of his letters from that period, Oskar was initially excited by with his replica of Alma ("even though its breasts and hips were stuffed with sawdust," as described by Weindinger), but Doll Alma was—no surprise—a disappointment when it came to whatever "activities" Oskar had in mind for it. Nevertheless he took his lemons and made lemonade: The doll could serve as a model, and he could still be the disappointed lover. He painted and drew the doll as obsessively as he had Alma.

It gets weirder. One month after receiving the Alma doll and, presumably, fully appreciating its inadequacies, Oskar attempted to contact flesh-and-blood Alma through a mutual friend who passed on the message that Oskar still loved her and wanted to reestablish contact. This last-ditch attempt didn't work either. Kokoschka couldn't have Alma in the flesh, and he decided shortly thereafter that he'd had his fill of Frau Mahler *die Puppe* (more commonly known among the OK circle as *die schweigsame Frau* (the silent woman). It was time to give her a fitting send-off, in a way that only the zany Oskar could host. "It had managed to cure me completely of my Passion," he wrote later. "So I gave a big champagne party with chamber music, during which Hulda

[Oskar's housekeeper] exhibited the doll in all its beautiful clothes for the last time. When dawn broke—I was quite drunk, as was everyone else—I beheaded it out in the garden and broke a bottle of red wine over its head." The question was and is, was this the performance art of an eccentric or the misogynistic retribution of an obsessed ex?

The next day policemen who saw the carnage in the garden through the gates busted into Oskar's house, suspecting that a real person had been killed in a crime of passion. Kokoschka fessed up: Yes, he had killed Alma the doll in cold blood. Despite this, Alma and OK exchanged occasional letters over the years.

Nearly a century after Kokoschka had his way with Doll Alma, a remarkable film called *Lars and the Real Girl* was released that

---

♥ Alma's Amours

Alma Mahler was a legend in her own time for being a cold, cruel, vain anti-Semite. She was also beautiful and brilliant and had an eclectic list of lovers:

- Gustav Klimt, painter of *The Kiss*, also Alma's first kiss
- Alexander Zemlinsky, composer/conductor and possessor of "virtuoso hands"
- Gustav Mahler, composer/conductor
- Walter Gropius, architect, founder of Bauhaus School, patient of Sigmund Freud
- Dr. Paul Kammerer, biologist and toad expert, who pledged to shoot himself at Mahler's grave if she didn't say "I do." (She didn't. He did shoot himself, however, fifteen years later, over a toad dispute.)
- Franz Werfel, writer, who was buried in a smoking jacket and silk shirt, with a second shirt to change, and his spectacles in his jacket pocket

stars a guy, his life-size love doll, and the community that comes to love and accept her. While the similarities between Oskar and Doll Alma and Lars and Bianca pretty much end there, for both Oskar and Lars the love for and the staged death of a doll are key to moving on.

Egon Schiele

In 1915 the Austrian artist Egon Schiele painted an homage to Oskar Kokoschka's *Bride of the Wind (The Tempest)*. In it, Schiele mimics the basic composition of *Bride of the Wind* (a big curve created by two bodies, surrounded by a lot of tangles) and the subject matter (a couple in an embrace), but where Oskar's painting is dark yet tender and suggests a postcoital nap, Egon's shouts implosion. The man, according to the catalogue raisonné of his work edited by Jane Kallir, "plants a vampire's mortal kiss, not tenderly on his lover's lips, but guiltily on her head." As the lovers clutch at each other, the image conveys fear of change and, maybe more so, the fear of escaping the comfortable trap of habit—a feeling that is pretty universal in relationships heading south.

The man in the painting is Schiele himself, and the woman is Valerie "Wally" Neuzil, his model for a number of his most striking paintings, and it literally and figuratively depicts a scene from their breakup. At the time he was twenty-five and she was twenty-one, and their affair was not a short one—she had been his model-cum-lover since they'd met in Vienna when she was seventeen. She had also seen him through some bad times, only to be cruelly cast off in favor of a "good girl."

No one knows much about Wally. She was described as having

striking red hair, and before she met Schiele, she modeled (and likely bedded) Gustav Klimt. She was a relatively uneducated *süsses Mädel* ("sweet young thing") with what contemporaries noted was a "queenly bearing" and striking features. She was, in the more-or-less fashion of any bohemian culture, a prostitute.

♥ Schiele Shock

Schiele painted and drew plenty of "ordinary" subjects like landscapes and portraits, but he's best known for his brazenly erotic images of nude women, himself, and couples, including homosexuals. His most aggressive work naturally horrified viewers with traditional tastes, but many critics and private collectors lapped it up. Naturally, the question arises as to whether or not, even now, Schiele's erotic work amounts to pornography, a point the *New York Times* weighed in on while reviewing a gallery show of his work:

"Was Schiele a pornographer? In some sense he surely was making art with the purpose of provoking sexual arousal—in addition to shocking the bourgeoisie—and there were people who purchased his work with that purpose in mind, so the answer is yes. (There is also enough evidence to get him charged, if not convicted, as a pedophile by today's standards.) But there have been few pornographers who drew as well as he did. . . . His ways with composition, line and color and his responsiveness to paper were nothing short of exquisite."

During their time together, Schiele tried to live the bohemian life with her (read: living together openly but not married), only to have it end in disaster. The first time, his neighbors in the beautiful medieval city of Krumau were horrified to catch a glimpse of a nude model posing out in his garden. For that, he and Wally were run out of town. Thinking that a tiny town would be more forgiving, the next year (1912), Schiele and Wally settled in Neulengbach to paint in peace. But then chaos struck again when a teenage girl showed up at their doorstep. Tatjana von Mossig had run away from home, and while Schiele and Wally appear simply to have been giving her compassionate shelter, he was accused by her father of kidnapping and sexually abusing her. Ultimately these charges were dropped, because Tatjana refused to testify against Schiele, but the authorities did get him for "public immorality"—they'd found brazenly erotic drawings and watercolors in his apartment (likely of Wally, but possibly of someone younger), and Tatjana had seen them. Schiele served a total of twenty-one days in jail—not a long sentence, but terrifying for him. Many of his patrons who had previously warned him to be very careful about using children and adolescents as subjects took an I-told-you-so attitude, and Schiele was shattered for months. Most Schiele specialists think that he was guilty of carelessness and naïveté more than any moral lapse, an interpretation perhaps informed by the fact that Wally stood by him through this difficult time.

Around 1914, Schiele and Wally went on the move again, settling into an apartment in the suburbs of Vienna. It wasn't too long before Schiele's eye started to wander around his new neighborhood. He soon found that he could see clearly into the apartment across the way, where sisters in their early twenties, Adele and Edith Harms, lived with their family. Determined to catch both their eyes, "he flapped his drawings out the window and made bizarre, provocative gestures," according to the Schiele expert Jane Kallir. Schiele had apparently learned from his mentor, Gustav Klimt, that using coarse dialect rather than High German, was another surefire method to attract upstanding young ladies. (We can only imagine that he entreated them with a modern-day equivalent of "Yo, baby, wanna come over?")

I'm not sure on whose judgment this reflects worse, Wally's or Schiele's, but apparently Schiele dispatched Wally to make friends with Edith and Adele. From there he started to meet them in secret, with twenty-one-year-old Wally as chaperone. By early 1915, Edith had fallen in love with him and he with her. "I am planning to get married—perhaps favorably, not to Wally," he wrote to a friend. Sure, Wally was hot and good in bed and loyal, but in Schiele's eyes she wasn't wife material.

The real problem, however, was that Schiele wanted to have his lady cake and eat it, too, by marrying Edith (who by this time objected to her friend Wally's "influence") but still keeping Wally on the side. After it was settled that he would marry Edith, Schiele met Wally in a coffeehouse and had the balls to present her with a quasilegal document that would obligate her to go on an annual holiday with him. Earlier in their relationship, he'd made her sign a statement attesting that she was not in love with him, but this took his nonmonogamist machinations to a new level. No doubt feeling utterly betrayed and outraged, Wally denied him his request and stomped out of his life forever.

Schiele's proposed arrangement with Wally could well have been inspired by the lifestyle his mentor, Gustav Klimt, shared with his longtime model and mistress, Emilie Flöge. Klimt never married her or anyone else, yet he fathered over a dozen illegitimate children with other women. This might explain why, when one looks closely at Klimt's glittering iconic painting *The Kiss*, one gets the feeling that the model (Emilie) isn't in the mood.

Schiele and Edith married on June 17, 1915. Schiele's mother, who had always been uncomfortable with Wally, welcomed Edith with open arms. Reportedly she stated that "Edith is a daughter-in-law such as I had dreamed of."

Three days after their wedding, Schiele began military service as a guard to prisoners of war, a post that allowed him to continue to draw even on the job. When Klimt died in 1918, Schiele assumed his laurels as Austria's leading artist. Edith contracted and died of Spanish flu later that year when she was six months pregnant, and Schiele died of the same illness three days after she did. His last works, created during those few days between their deaths, were sketches of Edith.

After her split with Schiele in 1915, Wally became a nurse with the Red Cross. In 1917 she contracted scarlet fever in Dalmatia and died. While she might have died in obscurity, posthumously she's become anything but obscure. Indeed, if there is a God, Wally just might have had the last laugh: Schiele's *Portrait of Wally* was one of the many works that were tied up in endless litigation when descendants of the painting's original owner claimed that before it reached the collection of the Leopold Museum in Austria, it had been plundered by the Nazis. In 2010 the Leopold Museum paid a staggering $19 million to the heirs of the original owner, thereby setting right a wrong of more than seventy years' standing.

The Museum of Broken Relationships

THE STORY MAY well be apocryphal, but I seem to remember reading way back when that shortly after her split with Brad Pitt in 2005, Jennifer Aniston built a bonfire on the beach outside her home in Malibu and burned every piece of lingerie he'd ever given her.

Once an intimate relationship ends, I think we all wind up evaluating every item in our lives that reminds us of the other person, thinking on a subconscious or conscious level, *Do I really want that in my life?* In the confusion we may make harried choices—cling to, hide, toss, or destroy?—regarding items that remind us of who and what we've lost. Often there isn't any apparent rhyme or reason to it. For well over a decade, I've held on to a cigarette roller from a guy I had a brief affair with overseas, even though I don't smoke and never saw him again. Then, after one long-term relationship ended, I was quite clear on what I kept and why: Deep in my basement, I still have a bookend he made for me, early on in our relationship, by pouring concrete into a mason jar and then breaking the jar (how apt!), but I was quick to pitch a chef's coat he'd given me our last Christmas together, by which point his gifts seemed to say more about his admiration for my pot roast than anything else.

Had I known about Olinka Vištica and Dražen Grubišić, however, I just might have sent the chef's coat their way. In 2003, at the end of their own relationship, when they were attempting to divvy up the many monetarily valueless artifacts they'd amassed, Olinka and Dražen, both artists, hit on the idea of creating an entire collection of artifacts from finito relationships. Over time what started as a traveling exhibition became what is now known as the Museum of Broken Relationships. It has become so successful that every year it crops up in the news on Valentine's Day, and in 2011 the European Museum of the Year Award recognized Olinka and Dražen's brainchild as the most innovative museum in Europe. "Found art" might have been all the rage with Picasso and his friends in the early twentieth century, but now the Museum of Broken Relationships just might have created a new tradition in what we could call "sent art." At this point, with thousands of items in its collection, the museum is effectively a collective monument to what it calls "brokenships."

♥ One Man's Trash . . .

A decade after its inception, the Museum of Broken Relationships has items in its collection that are . . . well, masterpieces. Many art museums have "mascots," like the Metropolitan Museum of Art's ancient Egyptian turquoise blue ceramic hippo known as William. The Museum of Broken Relationships' equivalent is a weathered (okay, drunk-looking) garden gnome called "Divorce Day Mad Dwarf," who is missing his nose, his left cheek, his knees, and part of his hat, apparently because he'd been hurled over a car and onto asphalt. His trip over the windshield of the car, according to the exhibit description, was a "short long arc [that] defined the end of love." Other famous items in the collection include a pair of handcuffs lined with pink fake fur, an axe once used to hack up an ex's furniture ("Ex Axe"), and a wedding dress from a nuptial celebration in Greece that had eight hundred guests but wound up in divorce.

The Museum of Broken Relationships continues to solicit donations, as it notes on its Web site: "Would you also like to become a donor? Recently ended a relationship? Wish to unburden the emotional load by erasing everything that reminds you of that painful experience? Don't do it—one day you will be sorry."

Take heed, Aniston, take heed.

· IV ·

FILM AND LITERATURE

GREAT LITERATURE AND films are like dressing rooms: In them we get to discreetly try misadventures of all cuts and colors on for size. Narrative allows us to gaze at ourselves in costumes of infidelity, suicide, madness, murder, and revenge. We can look without having to leap.

As far as heartbreak in film and literature goes, certain figures become touchstones, whether it's Kate Winslet and her mastery of the rash, reckless rush into good decisions and bad in the characters she plays, or Hemingway's famous "complicated" relationship with women both on the page and in real life, or the dangerous allure of Lord Byron. Through film and literature, we create shorthand for experience that anyone can read.

Then again, there's something to the fascination we have with the fact that people who create narrative—writers, directors, and actors—have their own private narratives that may or may not inform their work. We derive huge satisfaction from making the link between the public and the private, by at least trying to understand what they leave in, what they leave out, how they manipulate details, and why. In literature and film's best tales of heartbreak, as well as the biographies of our favorite writers, we spelunk for evidence that brilliance is spawned by firsthand experience. With heartbreak on the page or on-screen, authenticity is in the details.

A Hyena Takes a Lover

MARY WOLLSTONECRAFT'S EPITAPH might well have been SO VERY SMART, AND YET SO VERY STUPID. Often called the world's first feminist, she's best known for her breakout work from 1792, *A Vindication of the Rights of Woman*, which laid out the founding principles of feminist thought: that women are as capable as men when it comes to rational thought, that women have the right to be educated, and that educated women better society as a whole. She rattled off the work in just six weeks, but since she'd grown up in a violent home, was unmarried, and had supported herself by teaching, writing, and editing for years, it's fair to say that she had stewed in its content for decades before putting pen to paper. *Vindication* was an instant bestseller in Mary's native England, critics loved it, and she became famous and influential overnight. One aristocratic lady known for her meekness cautioned her husband, "I have been reading *The Rights of Woman*, so you must in future expect me to be very tenacious in my rights and privileges."

Many of us have been taught that *A Vindication of the Rights of Woman* was greeted with shock and outrage. Maybe to a certain degree, but a good chunk of the ire seems to have been generated by one Horace Walpole, a Tory earl who called Wollstonecraft "a hyena in petticoats" and lumped her in with the terrifying likes of Thomas Paine (author of *The Age of Reason* and *Rights of Man*) and other "philosophizing serpents." So bloated was Walpole's sense of self, before his death he bade his legal team to fill up a chest with his *3-million-word* memoir. Strangely, only fragments of it have been published (much less read), while Mary's quite brief *Vindication*, the work he so derided, has been reprinted and commented on countless times.

But the thing about Mary Wollstonecraft that is so intriguing is the mismatch between her inherent wisdom about the politics of gender and the wild misjudgments that characterized her relationships with men. For all her brilliance, she appears to have nourished herself with a curious broth made of chutzpah and plain old naïveté.

Wollstonecraft's biographer Claire Tomalin suggests that Mary's first significant romantic intrigue came in the form of Henry Fuseli, a painter of Swiss origin who lived in London. When they first met, he was a forty-seven-year-old who was well seasoned in indiscretion and she was a virginal twenty-nine. She adored "the grandeur of his soul, that quickness of comprehension, and lovely sympathy," and they flirted wildly in a sort of push-pull dynamic— he'd tease her with brazen talk about sex, and she'd write him letters, many of which he left unopened in his pocket. On her end it was surely thrilling to connect with such a naughty man, and on his it was a delight to flirt with a woman who was the very opposite of his wife, Sophie, an uneducated model.

In August 1792, with an instant bestseller to her name and cash to spare, Mary tore herself away from Fuseli and set off to Paris with a party of friends who, like her, wanted to be where the action was. When they reached Dover, however, news from the City of Light forced them to turn back. The Tuileries Palace and been stormed, over six hundred Swiss Guards had been massacred in the process, and King Louis XVI had been arrested. Even for those sympathetic to the revolution, Paris was clearly not a safe place to be.

Mary returned to London, and, perhaps coping with the letdown of the cancellation of the trip and feeling a bit adrift, she paid a . . . shall we say surprising visit to Sophie Fuseli, Henry's wife. As Tomalin delicately puts it, Mary asked that she "be admitted to the household on a permanent basis," so that she could see the man whom she regarded as her spiritual partner every day. In short, she wanted what might be called a one-third-platonic ménage à trois. Sophie flew into a rage and threw Mary out. Without a plan or a lover, Mary headed for Paris again, by herself this time, in December 1792. While she wouldn't be the first woman to set off into a war zone in an attempt to forget her broken heart, and she certainly wouldn't be the last, you have to remember that by this point Robespierre had declared that "Louis must die, so that the country may live." If anything, Paris was even more horrific a scene than it had been a few months earlier when she'd turned back from Dover.

Needless to say, Paris midrevolution wasn't the romantic experience that she'd imagined: Every day she saw King Louis escorted back and forth from his prison to his trial. Before long, however, mad love made it all worth it.

The Slippery Gilbert Imlay

If one were to write a romance novel set in the late eighteenth century featuring an unscrupulous and uncaring rogue, it would be hard to come up with a better name for him than "Gilbert

Imlay." When Mary first met the real-life incarnation of this cad, she didn't like him, but soon enough she was in love. Gilbert was a writer from New Jersey who had served in the American Revolution (surely an attractive history for a radical like Mary), and all he wanted, he said, was a farm in the American wilderness and a passel of kids—the perfect noble-savage routine to lure in a woman with a penchant for adventure. His declaration that he considered marriage a corrupt institution must have been music to Mary's ears, for in *The Vindication of the Rights of Woman* she had called marriage "legal prostitution." He flattered her no end—something she wasn't accustomed to—and she drank it in and was transformed into a self-assured, lighthearted woman who believed she had found her soul mate. As Claire Tomalin observed, "Women who have gone to great lengths to raise themselves above the ordinary level of their sex are likely to believe, for a while at any rate, that they will be loved the more ardently and faithfully for their pains."

In the spring of 1793, Mary and Gilbert started a steamy affair, and by September, just when the Reign of Terror was starting, she was pregnant. In what looks like his only noble act, Gilbert registered Mary as his wife with the American embassy, so she'd have the protections of an American citizen. Then he took off on business to Le Havre, leaving Mary behind to gestate to the sound track of mass executions of the revolution's enemies, including King Louis and Marie Antoinette.

That winter, alone in Paris, Mary threw herself into writing *A Historical and Moral View of the French Revolution*, but before long the surrounding violence coupled with the infrequency of letters from Gilbert got to her. Halfway through her pregnancy, she took a carriage 125 miles to join him in Le Havre. There she finished her book and gave birth to a baby girl, whom she named Fanny. For two months or so, they appear to have been a happy little family; Mary adored tending to her newborn and wrote to a friend, "My little Girl begins to suck so MANFULLY that her father reckons saucily on her writing the second part of the Rights of Woman!"

But it seems domestic bliss, at least the kind that included a loving mother and an infant, bored Gilbert. In July 1794, he announced to Mary that he needed to go to London on business; he would send for her shortly. It was nearly a year before she did join him there, and then of course her worst fears were confirmed: He had taken up with someone else.

When it was clear that Gilbert had deserted her, Mary attempted suicide with laudanum (see p. 198). Then Gilbert asked her to go to Scandinavia as his business envoy to sort out a deal that had gone wrong. Call it perverse or call it resourceful, but either way it takes guts to send your recently dumped mistress to a strange land when she's just attempted suicide and is tending to your infant so she can recoup your financial losses while you stay at home with your girlfriend.

Just as Mary failed to see through Gilbert's supremely avoidant ways, she also failed to detect the sketchiness of his business affairs. When he told her that he wanted to return to America to live in the wilderness, he left out the fact that he'd left behind so much debt from land speculation there that if he were to return, he'd immediately be hit with a massive lawsuit. Moreover, while he led his expat clique to believe that he was in Paris as a diplomat, in reality he was there to make bank as a blockade runner. So when he dispatched Mary to Scandinavia to track down a ship he'd bought right around when Fanny was born, it stands to reason that he didn't reveal that it was fraudulently registered and that it wasn't loaded with ballast (dense material used to stabilize a vessel that is not carrying cargo), but rather with silver and plate, some even inscribed with the Bourbon arms—in other words, a rather dangerous fortune.

In the summer of 1795, Mary dutifully set off for Sweden, Norway, and Denmark, with her one-year-old daughter and a nursemaid, Marguerite, in tow. What became of her negotiations on Gilbert's behalf and of the treasure ship are completely unclear, but while she was traveling, she wrote a series of letters to Gilbert that are astonishingly beautiful and before long became a prototype for the romantic and contemplative accounts of lonely journeys popularized by Byron, Shelley, Wordsworth, and Coleridge. An example, from her first letter of the trip:

> Nothing, in fact, can equal the beauty of the northern summer's evening and night, if night it may be called that only wants the glare of day, the full light which frequently seems so impertinent, for I could write at midnight very well without a candle. I contemplated all Nature at rest; the rocks, even grown darker in their appearance, looked as if they partook of the general repose, and reclined more heavily on their foundation. "What," I exclaimed, "is this active principle which keeps me still awake? Why fly my thoughts abroad, when everything around me appears at home?"

The trip appears to have had a healing affect on Mary, but when she returned to London, Gilbert didn't meet her and made it clear that he'd moved on for good with an actress. Once again the very notions she'd crusaded for—freedom and the idea that marriage was no more than a tether—had stabbed her in the back, leaving her to fend for herself.

Mary dashed off a letter to Gilbert, writing, "Let my wrongs sleep with me! Soon, very soon, I shall be at peace. When you receive this, my burning head will be cold. . . . I shall plunge into the Thames where there is least chance of my being snatched from the death I seek. God bless you! May you never know by experience what you have made me endure. Should your sensibility ever awake, remorse will find its way to your heart; and, in the midst of business and sensual pleasure, I shall appear before you, the victim of your deviation from rectitude."

She then left baby Fanny and Marguerite and went down to the Thames, hired a boat, and rowed to Putney Bridge, which she promptly jumped off. Fortunately, some boatmen saw her and pulled her out, unconscious but alive.

Gilbert did make sure she was escorted to her lodgings, but he didn't visit her in deference to his mistress. Then, apparently after he hinted that he was no longer in love with said mistress, Mary dusted off her "Let's live in a ménage à trois" proposal, only to be rejected yet again.

Go Your Own Way

Finally Mary was ready to move on and return to what she really was best at: making her own way. In 1796 she gathered and published the letters she had sent from Scandinavia under the title *Letters Written in Sweden, Norway, and Denmark*, which sold well and which critics loved.

Among her fans was William Godwin, a journalist and political philosopher who in 1794 had written the world's first thriller, *Things as They Are; or, The Adventures of Caleb Williams*. Of Mary's *Letters* he later wrote, in a recounting of her life story, "If ever there was a book calculated to make a man in love with its author, this appears to me to be the book. She speaks of her sorrows, in a way that fills us with melancholy, and dissolves us in tenderness, at the same time that she displays a genius which commands all our admiration."

After a careful courtship, passionate love erupted between William and Mary, and she was again pregnant. This time she conceded that marriage would at least assure their child legitimacy (having learned the hard way that this was important, given that Gilbert did nothing for Fanny). They took their vows in March 1797, when she was about three months pregnant. William and Mary lived in adjoining houses contentedly, often communicating during the day by letter so that each might write in peace.

This is one of those stories that you really, really wish would end with "and they lived happily ever after." Unfortunately, it doesn't. Mary gave birth to her second daughter, named Mary, at the end of August 1797, and died ten days later of puerperal fever. William was of course devastated and wrote a friend, "I firmly believe there does not exist her equal in the world. I know from experience we were formed to make each other happy. I have not the least expectation that I can ever know happiness again."

Three years later, meaning it as a loving memorial to his wife, William published *Memoirs of the Author of A Vindication of the Rights of Woman*. In it he revealed what many thought was too much: that both her children were in some measure illegitimate, the nitty-gritty of her interactions with Fuseli and Imlay, and, worst of all, her suicide attempts. One contemporary critic of the memoir ventured that William showed "the want of all feeling in stripping his dead wife naked." About four years later, he remarried.

With respect to Mary's progeny, there again lies some bad news. Her daughter Fanny committed suicide in 1816, at the age of twenty-two. But her daughter Mary, so like her mother, eloped with Percy Bysshe Shelley, an advocate of free love who abandoned his family to be with her and later subsidized the Godwin family. Mary went on to write *Frankenstein*.

When William Godwin remarried, his daughter Mary gained a stepsister her same age, Claire Clairmont. As a voluptuous and charming teenager, Claire briefly attracted the attentions of the louche Lord Byron. Their liaison produced a daughter, Allegra, whom Claire reluctantly turned over to Byron. Byron then, much to Claire's horror, placed Allegra in a convent, where the little girl died at age five. As if that weren't enough drama for one person, Claire was also very tight with Mary and Percy Bysshe Shelley, to the point where she ran away with them when they eloped, and many of their contemporaries (including Byron) believed that *they* lived in a ménage à trois and that Shelley was father of Claire's second child, Elena. For years scholars assumed that Claire supported Mary and Percy's free-love philosophy, but in 2010 a fragment of a memoir she wrote in her seventies surfaced, revealing that at least at the end of her life (or maybe after her conversion to Catholicism) she felt that the philosophy of free love "abused affections that should be the solace and balm of life" and made "monsters" of both Byron and Shelley. Byron, who once called her a "little fiend," she specifically compared to "a human tyger slaking his thirst for inflicting pain upon defenceless women."

Mad, Bad, and Dangerous to Know

ANY WOMAN WHO sends her estranged lover a bloody lock of her pubic hair deserves a medal—I'm just not sure for what. Even by the standards of London during the Regency, when over-the-top drama was par for the course, Lady Caroline Lamb (1785–1828) pulled out all the stops when it came to her pursuit of the seasoned womanizer Lord Byron. In short, she had the fine art of stalking down pat. Caroline was like Marianne Dashwood, the semi-stalker sister from *Sense and Sensibility* on steroids; indeed, it's not a stretch to imagine that she read the Jane Austen novel and took notes shortly before she met Byron.

When Caroline first caught sight of Byron in the spring of 1812, she'd already written him an anonymous fan letter (he'd just published the first installment of *Childe Harold's Pilgrimage*, his breakthrough narrative poem that had ensured that aristocratic women were falling all over him). But rather than throw herself at him, she turned her back on him and marched out the door—a strategy that of course immediately piqued his interest. Based on that first encounter, she observed that he was "mad, bad, and dangerous to know" (a prescient phrase that was just as descriptive of her as it was of him). According to Paul Douglass's biography of Caroline, within what appears to be a matter of weeks, they were having a torrid affair.

Lady Caroline had always been a loose cannon, even as a child. She'd spent much of her early years living under the roof of her fashionable aunt, Georgiana Cavendish, Duchess of Devonshire, who modeled extremism in her own private life. Before she even hit puberty, Lady Caroline was so volatile and reckless that she was medicated with the opium-based sedative laudanum. When she was nineteen, she married William Lamb, an aspiring politician of appropriate rank whom she also loved, an amazing feat in their milieu. Two years later they had a son who was apparently autistic. Most aristocratic families then sent off children with severe disabilities to live at institutions, but, tellingly, the Lambs cared for young George at home until he died.

♥ Book Alert!

Georgiana, Duchess of Devonshire, by Amanda Foreman

One of the most dramatic and powerful women of the Regency was Georgiana, Duchess of Devonshire. She had it all—money, beauty, brains, and considerable behind-the-scenes political power—but also more than her fair share of tragedy and poor judgment. Amanda Foreman's biography of her is top-notch, capturing her allure and piecing together how this remarkable woman (ancestor to Princess Diana as well as Sarah, Duchess of York) wielded power in fashion, society, and politics and pulled off living for years in a shocking ménage à trois with her husband and her best friend.

Much as she was a devoted mother at home, Caroline was high society's wild card. She wore her hair short, sported dresses with necklines that nearly revealed her nipples, and flirted with abandon. While Byron was initially shocked by, or perhaps even intimidated by, her outré eccentricities, she was the first woman he was ever involved with who engaged him intellectually. The hundreds of letters that they exchanged over the course of less than six months are testament not just to mad passion but to the shared interests of two voracious readers.

Of course, passion like that never lasts. Within just a few months, Byron seems to have been both irritated and bored by her and frustrated that she wouldn't say that she loved him more than she did her husband. "My God, you shall pay for this, I'll wring that obstinate little heart," he told her.

So began one of the ugliest kinds of breakups—the long ones garnished with hysteria. Byron left London in part to avoid Caroline, but she continued to fire off passionate letters begging for his attention. When he returned to London, she showed up at his rooms unannounced and disguised as a page, and when Byron's best friend told her to leave, she tried to stab herself with a knife.

In August, at most five months after they'd started carrying on, she sent him the aforementioned token of her love, referring to herself as not just his "wild antelope" but as "Caroline Byron." Her letter read, "I asked you not to send blood but Yet do—because if it means love I like to have it. I cut the hair too close & bled much more than you need—do not you the same & pray put not scissors near where *quei capelli* [those hairs] grow—sooner take it from the arm or wrist—pray be careful."

♥ Mother's Little Helper, Nineteenth-Century Style

As Elizabeth Kerri Mahon points out in her book *Scandalous Women: The Lives and Loves of History's Most Notorious Women*, if Lady Caroline Lamb lived today, her charm coupled with her erratic and inappropriate behavior might well result in a diagnosis of bipolar disorder and a prescription for a mood stabilizer such as lithium or Depakote. Two hundred years ago, however, she was likely deemed to be suffering from "erotomania" and dosed with laudanum, an opium tincture (10 percent opium dissolved in 90 percent alcohol) that typically included not just the requisite poppy product but also sherry, cinnamon, and saffron, all flavors that masked opium's native bitterness. Throughout the nineteenth century and even into the twentieth, laudanum was the panacea for any number of complaints, including moodiness or depression, insomnia, edema, nausea, menstrual cramps, and probably even the vague boredom that marked the existences of many upper-class women. When the pale, lackluster complexion of a tuberculosis patient became fashionable among the Victorians, some women even took laudanum for cosmetic reasons, making it what today would be a cocktail of Midol, Xanax, lithium, Ambien, Dramamine, and self-tanner. Terrifyingly, variations on opium tinctures were also commonly used on active children and even colicky infants; one could say it was the era's Ritalin. And because medical standards at the time maintained that no cure could be addictive, many a junkie was made.

Shortly thereafter he met with her and insisted that she go to Ireland to protect both of their reputations. She went unwillingly, and then, once he was more or less "safe" from her, for a time he continued to write her gracious, even loving, letters. But within a few months, Byron had taken up with Jane Harley, Countess of Oxford and Caroline's friend, who was sixteen years his senior and had six children who were christened "the Harleian Miscellany" by contemporary jesters because their paternity was so uncertain.

Byron noted that Jane's "autumnal charms" were a perfect fit for him, and with respect to Caroline, Jane was an accomplished mean girl, albeit a forty-year-old one. Together Byron and Jane composed and dispatched letters to Caroline, complete with a seal bearing Jane's initials. Witness this doozy from November 1812, just two or three months after Caroline left to take a break in Ireland:

> I am no longer your lover; and since you oblige me to confess it, by this truly unfeminine persecution, learn that I am attached to another, whose name it would of course be dishonorable to mention. I shall ever remember with gratitude the many instances I have received the predilection you have shewn in my favor. I shall ever continue your friend if your Ladyship will permit me so to style myself; and as a first proof of my regard, I offer you this advice, correct your vanity, which is ridiculous; exert your absurd caprices upon others; and leave me in peace.

Upon her return to London, Caroline was understandably distressed. Already thin, she lost weight, and Byron commented to a friend that he was "haunted by a skeleton." When they saw each other at society functions, she managed to keep it together, but that Christmas of 1812 she made a bonfire at the country home of her relations and bade village girls dressed in white to dance while she tossed copies of Byron's letters and keepsakes into the fire. She even torched an effigy of her former lover as her page recited, "Burn, fire, burn, while wondering boys explain / And gold and trinkets glitter in the flame"—a couplet she wrote just for the occasion.

The situation got still nastier and Caroline still more erratic and delusional. She tricked his publisher into giving her a miniature portrait of Byron and then requested a lock of his hair. Byron responded by sending her a lock of Jane's hair instead. His family motto was *"Crede Byron"* (Trust Byron); she went to the trouble of having her buttons inscribed with NO CREDE BYRON. In the summer of 1813, roughly a year after the peak of their affair, they crossed paths at a masked ball, traded barbs, and she wound up cutting herself with a knife, an incident that London's newspapers relished reporting.

By 1815, Byron needed to get married in order to save both his reputation and his financial troubles, and a respectable heiress by the name of Annabella Milbanke was just the ticket: She was prim and religious, and she also took particular delight in math, leading Byron to nickname her the "princess of parallelograms." Perhaps best of all, she was Caroline's cousin.

Thanks to shrewd self-promotion, Byron was one of the first modern celebrities, and his wife even coined the term "Byromania" to connote the fervor he generated, particularly among women. If he lived now, he'd be the equivalent of a rock star and a PETA supporter to boot, à la R.E.M.'s Michael Stipe: When he was a student at Trinity and dogs were forbidden, he kept a pet bear. Over the course of his lifetime his menagerie reportedly included not just the upper-class requisite horses and dogs, but a parrot, an eagle, a crow, a falcon, an Egyptian crane, a heron, a crocodile, a fox, a badger, a goat with a broken leg, peacocks, geese, guinea hens, cats, and four monkeys, many of which lived indoors. The poet fearlessly nursed his rabies-afflicted dog Boatswain until the dog died; he then ordered that a marble monument to mark the dog's grave be built on his estate, Newstead Abbey, where it still stands today.

To say that this was a bad fit would be an understatement. Annabella quickly produced a child, but Byron's saturnine moods made her fear for her safety. The moment that separation was in the air, Caroline swept in with damning evidence of his immorality. Byron, Caroline alleged, had told her when they'd last met that he'd had an incestuous relationship with his half sister, Augusta, adding that that was why *she* had broken up with *him*. Armed with accusations of incest, and tacking on her own accusation of sodomy, Annabella had everything she needed to get a divorce on her terms. When Byron suspected that Caroline was behind the incest allegations, she had the audacity to reply not only that *she*, not he, was the one falsely accused but that she would die to save him.

In the wake of the scandal, Byron fled to Europe, never to return to England again. He died in Greece in 1824. Annabella never married again and devoted herself to liberal causes such as abolition of slavery and prison reform.

Caroline flamboyantly milked the drama. In 1816, right on the heels of Byron's downfall in England, she published *Glenarvon*, a roman à clef in which the main character is described as scornful and nasty, plus guilty of the ultimate criminal trifecta: incest, murder, and infanticide. So bold was Caroline in *Glenarvon* that she actually included, word for word, the cruel letter that Byron and Lady Oxford had composed and sent to her. The book sold out, and Byron noted to his publisher, "Kiss and tell, bad as it is, is surely somewhat less than ∗∗∗∗ and publish."

The Three Horses of the Heartbreak Apocalypse: Worst-Case Scenarios

THE LITERATURE QUIZ: How well do you know your nineteenth-century heartbroken heroines? Match the following characters with their fates:

1. Your lover left you at the altar, skipping town with a fair chunk of your fortune.
2. You read so many romance novels that you think your life is supposed to resemble one.
3. A man rapes you, and the guy you subsequently fall in love with can't seem to understand that it wasn't your fault.
4. You fall in love with a guy who is not your husband, and in order to be with him, you have to give up your children as well as the respect of anyone who has ever known you.

A. Suicide
B. Never getting over it
C. Suicide
D. Murder and execution

I think many of you know where I'm going here, but if you're not familiar with certain nineteenth-century novels involving the sweetest dairymaid on the planet, a shut-in spinster, a licentious Frenchwoman, or an aristocratic wife who falls in love with a fellow named Vronsky, you're missing out on some of literature's classic heartbreak stories (not to mention the opportunity to thank your lucky stars that divorce and meds are now viable options).

Suicide

Suicide in literature is as old as the hills, but it's an especially common fate for one type of heroine in particular: the adulteress.

Suicide #1: *Madame Bovary* (1856)

First, a fabulously reductionist synopsis: Girl meets Boy #1, who is a drip to the nth degree. Girl marries Boy #1. Terribly bored with married life, Girl flirts with Boy #2. Boy #2 moves away, so Girl starts indiscreet affair with Boy #3, who is above her station. Girl spends ridiculous amounts of money attempting to match his station. Boy #3 dumps her. Girl runs into Boy #2 again, and after a steamy session in a closed carriage (a daylong extravaganza that requires Boy #2 to shout, "Keep going!" to the coachman multiple times) begins a lengthy affair with him that requires that she (a) spend even more money (love nests are so expensive!) and (b) lead a double life. Girl accrues enormous debt. Girl is financially ruined. Girl gobbles up arsenic, thinking she'll have a pleasant, romantic death. Ha!

More than ten years after *Madame Bovary* was published, a cartoon that is famous to this day depicted "Gustave Flaubert dissecting Madame Bovary," in which a mustachioed Flaubert in scrubs waves Emma Bovary's heart aloft, torchlike but skewered on a knife and dripping blood. The cartoon makes me chuckle, but it also prompted me to ask, was Emma Bovary ever really in love, or was she a love addict?

Some people think that Flaubert's writing so defies translation that it's impossible to really understand his work in English, but I think that even in translation it's clear that Emma suffers from a textbook case of love addiction. Not only that, Emma was not so much in love with Rodolphe Boulanger (Boy #3) or Léon Dupuis (Boy #2) as besotted with the second lives they seemingly furnished her. They were merely accessories to her extravagant fantasy life. And while disappointment in love and dissatisfaction with the realities of marriage in some measure drive her to suicide, what finally pushes her over the edge is financial ruin—the fact is that when it comes to aiding and abetting her own ridiculously romantic notions with material goods, the jig is up.

♥ Film Alert!

The 1991 film adaptation of *Madame Bovary*, starring the lovely and appropriately pinched and pale Isabelle Huppert, is definitely worth watching. Sure, the filmmaking is just plain gorgeous, but the suicide scene is truly over the top: She basically vomits pitch. The 2006 film *Little Children*, starring Kate Winslet, riffs on *Madame Bovary* in a few ways, including the boring marriage and the hot illicit sex. Memorable moments include Kate Winslet's character, Sarah, defending Madame Bovary to a gaggle of neighborhood matrons in a book club meeting.

When you look closely at Emma's suicide, it screams "impulsive" and "naïve." Clearly, Emma thinks that suicide will be sufficiently dramatic but painless, romantic but not messy—a fitting finale to her oh-so-tragic life. But no. She scarfs down arsenic, of all things, which makes for a long, excruciating, and downright gory death, complete with vomiting blood. Arguments over whether Flaubert was or wasn't a moralist abound, but in the end Emma's suicide bears a faint aftertaste of just deserts: If ever a character deserves to be told, "You made your bed, now lie in it" (or die in it, as the case may be), it just might be Emma Bovary. Still, given that Emma leaves a trail of wreckage behind her—her husband, her father, and her daughter are all destroyed—Flaubert is clearly not casting a vote in favor of the ultimate mortal sin.

Suicide #2: *Anna Karenina* (Published in Serial 1873–77)

Anna Karenina is a labyrinth of heartbreak: The novel opens with an emotionally destroyed Dolly, Anna's sister-in-law, whose husband cheated on her with the governess; its main plot picks apart Anna's abandonment of her husband and son in favor of mad love for Count Vronsky, a cavalry officer; and its subplot revolves around Levin, a gentleman farmer, and the tortured love he has for the debutante Kitty, who at first turns him down because she digs Vronsky and then is tormented by second thoughts when she recognizes that Vronsky is a cad and Levin is a catch.

We've Come a Long Way, Baby could be the modern subtitle to *Anna Karenina*, so important are divorce laws to the plot and its no-way-out conclusion. If a similar plot unfolded today, it would be resolved relatively simply, with Anna leaving her husband, getting a divorce, marrying Vronsky, sharing custody of her child with her ex-husband, and living more or less happily ever after. Not so easy in nineteenth-century Russia, when divorce laws required that one of three conditions be met in order for an unhappy couple to end their marriage: One of the spouses had to be physically disabled (nice!), missing for five years (reasonable), or a proven adulterer (as in caught either confessing or being caught in flagrante delicto by a third party). There was no option for a couple who wanted to separate with grace and respect and marry others better suited to them—what would now be called a no-fault divorce. Someone had to be the bad guy, either in truth or by faking it. What's worse, whoever was the adulterer gave up all rights to any children the couple might have. Divorce laws were so vicious that even if a woman left her husband and had a child with another man, that child belonged to her husband. So in Anna's situation, if she and Karenin divorced, she'd lose not only her child by Karenin but that by Vronsky as well.

Given that it was a loser-loses-all situation, no wonder Anna threw herself under a train in what has to be the creepiest, most drawn-out suicide in all literature. A cacophony of revelations spins through the eerie mock clarity that supposedly characterizes the moments before suicide. Anna finally sees that Vronsky is vain, and she muses on the mismatch between their feelings—the more she wants him, the less he wants her: "We walked to meet each other up to the time of our love, and then we have been irresistibly drifting in different directions." One of the things that's so remarkable about the scene is how trippy it is: Faces of passersby seem to leer at her, and everyone is repulsive, as if she's having a sudden and violent allergic reaction. It's like a 3-D rendering of a Munch painting.

The last details of Tolstoy's exacting portrait of suicide are worth looking at closely. As she calculates where to place herself with respect to the front and back wheels of the train car, Anna thinks, "There . . . in the very middle, and I will punish him and escape from everyone and from myself." She crosses herself. At the last instant—too late—she thinks, "Where am I? What am I doing? What for?" and tries to get up. Her final moments are vague and impressionistic, unlike the lucidity of the minutes before. "And the light by which she read the book filled with troubles, false-hoods, sorrow, and evil, flared up more brightly than ever before, lighted up for her all that had been in darkness, flickered, began to grow dim, and was quenched forever."

The question, of course, is whether suicide was really and truly Anna's only way out—whether it was at least somewhat *understandable*. Given the ins and outs of divorce in her milieu, it was— she is an utterly ruined woman in the eyes of her society. But Tolstoy clearly wasn't casting a vote for it either.

Never Getting Over It

If you ever got dumped at the altar, been financially ruined by an ex who stole your money and ran, or have a vendetta against cake, then Miss Havisham from Charles Dickens's 1861 novel *Great Expectations* is your girl. She's the ultimate jilted bride and perhaps the most memorable, eccentric figure in all of English literature: Not only does she launch a campaign of peculiar revenge that will last for decades, but she never leaves her house again, nor does she allow the celebratory meal, including the wedding cake, to be cleared. Moreover, assuming she's in her fifties when she first has young Pip brought to her house, as Dickens's notes for the novel suggest, and if we estimate that she was slated to marry at twenty-five, then one of the most memorable Havisham details is that she wears her wedding dress, underclothes, and stockings nonstop for almost thirty years.

Miss Havisham's dedication to her own grief is so intense that she disengages from the passage of time—the only real cure for the heartbroken—by stopping all the clocks in her house to mark the moment she received a letter from her groom announcing he wasn't going to make it. "I know nothing of days of the week; I know nothing of weeks of the year," she tells Pip. It's a contortionist move, when you really stop to think about it. Imagine stopping all one's clocks to forever mark one's unhappiest moment while one is in the midst of it—it shows a remarkable, almost improbable consciousness of the future at a time when one is most definitely consumed by the present. It's as if the present and the future, which flow into each other, suddenly become stuck together with super-glue. Moreover, stopping the clocks isn't just about stopping time, of memorializing a moment to the point of freezing the future. It's about being so preoccupied by sorrow that it doesn't matter if it's 8:00 AM or 4:00 PM—a state that sounds suspiciously like one of addiction.

The character of Miss Havisham was perhaps inspired by an Australian woman, Eliza Emily Donnithorne (1827–86), whose groom abandoned her on her wedding day in 1846. Like her fictional twin, Miss Donnithorne became a shut-in and left her wedding cake to rot on the table. If it is the case that Miss Donnithorne was a prototype, then Dickens likely heard of her through a friend who had relocated to Australia. One James Payne, a lesser-known novelist, claimed to have tipped Dickens off to the story and said that Dickens's version was "not one whit exaggerated."

Murder and Execution

I once read that Thomas Hardy's portrait of Tess Durbeyfield, the well-intentioned, utterly victimized heroine of his great master-piece *Tess of the d'Urbervilles*, is so painstaking and so compassion-ate that it's as if Hardy were her Pygmalion, utterly in love with his own creation (not an analysis anyone ventures about Flaubert's re-lationship with Emma or Tolstoy's with Anna, and certainly not Dickens's with Miss Havisham). As the critic Irving Howe once noted, "Tess is that rare creature in literature: goodness made interesting."

As far as the story goes, the most salient plot points are that teenage Tess is raped by a man named Alec, and several years later, the man she loves, Angel, abandons her when she shares with him her agony. Over and over again in the novel, she tries to do the honest and noble thing, whether that means baptizing her bastard child herself, trying to alert Angel by letter of her history before their wedding, or obeying his order that they must separate. Ultimately her frustration at not getting anywhere with that strategy transmogrifies into murder.

Full disclosure: *Tess* is one of my favorite novels. I think it ranks so high, that Tess resonates with me, much as I can't identify with the grim details of her life, because she means so very well, yet her life is frankly shit. Hardy's subtitle for *Tess of the d'Urbervilles* was *A Pure Woman Faithfully Presented*, but for the modern reader *Nice Girls Finish Last* might be more suitable.

Unlike Emma, Anna, and the divine Miss H., each of whom could have stopped their descents at various points along the way, it's only at the very end, when rage drives her to madness, that Tess makes a *decision* that triggers the final tragedy. When faced with love gone wrong, we all have our moments of self-recrimination where we search for the tipping point: *When was I too pushy? Too manipulative? Too presumptuous?* But in examining Tess's many moments of self-recrimination, it's hard to imagine what she could have come up with.

Many readers take issue with what they see as Tess's passivity (why didn't she *fight* for Angel, and why didn't she *fight off* Alec when he finds her again?), but I don't see it as passivity, rather as modesty. So entrenched is she in a social order where she's on the bottom rung, so determined is she to be honorable, so seriously does she take being a good person, that self-saving aggressiveness just isn't an option. Her goodness never pays off.

This, I think, is something many of us struggle with when heartbreak bangs at the door—how can our lives become such a mess when we are fundamentally well-intentioned? How can someone leave us when all we wanted was for that person to be happy? How can a relationship implode, and we wind up alone, when being generous was our modus operandi? Why are we spurned when all along we thought the relationship brought out the best in us?

In love and elsewhere, this is one of the toughest lessons we have to learn, often over and over again: No one ever said life was fair.

♥ Film Alert!

There's no shortage of great film versions of *Tess*. Check out Roman Polanski's 1979 adaptation, starring the sixteen-year-old Nastassja Kinski (whom Polanski, who was forty-three at the time, reportedly seduced); the 1998 miniseries version, starring Justine Waddell (who also played Estella to Charlotte Rampling's Miss Havisham in 1999); and the 2008 BBC interpretation, starring Gemma Arterton, who has also played Elizabeth Bennet in *Lost in Austen*, a completely silly and fun variation on *Pride and Prejudice*. The last version stars Eddie Redmayne and Hans Matheson respectively as Angel and Alec.

But in the end when you look at these fictional women collectively and think about who created them, it has to be said that they are all women as *men* imagined them, complete with male assumptions about just what a woman with a broken heart will do. Much as Flaubert, Dickens, Tolstoy, and Hardy clearly felt tremendous empathy for the plights of their characters specifically and for women generally, there is no truly feminine triumph in their tales. With the exception of Catherine Earnshaw in Emily Brontë's *Wuthering Heights*, the most enduring heartbroken heroines created by women of the nineteenth century—think Jane Eyre and Marianne and Eleanor Dashwood from *Sense and Sensibility*—are survivors.

The Painted Veil

O NE OF MY favorite novels about heartbreak, W. Somerset Maugham's *The Painted Veil*, brilliantly captures the complete arc of heartbreak: the mad love, the devastating breakup, the endless rumination, the reaching out to friends and subsequent reality check, and then the light at the end of the tunnel. It's a portrait of someone who suffers through heartbreak but comes out the other side a better person.

First a quick plot synopsis: Kitty, a silly young woman, lackadaisically marries Walter, a bacteriologist. Together they go to Hong Kong, where Kitty is utterly bored and begins a torrid affair with Charles, a dashing diplomat. After months of declaring his undying love, Charles announces to Kitty that he has no intentions of divorcing his wife and marrying her; she is destroyed by his betrayal. Fully aware of his wife's transgression, Walter forces her to accompany him to a village in the interior of China. There she settles into textbook self-recrimination and obsessive thinking:

> Her pain was so great that she could have screamed at the top of her voice; she had never known that one could suffer so much; and she asked herself desperately what she had done to deserve it. She could not make out why Charlie did

not love her: it was her fault, she supposed, but she had done everything she knew to make him fond of her. They had always got on so well, they laughed all the time they were together, they were not only lovers but good friends. She could not understand; she was broken. She told herself that she hated and despised him; but she had no idea how she was going to live if she was never to see him again.

This passage so perfectly captures not just the volatile, exquisite pain and confusion of heartbreak but how, after we've been dumped, we skewer ourselves with excruciating questions, asking ourselves, *What did I do wrong?* as we relive moments of the relationship, excavating mere seconds for clues.

> ### ♥ Film Alert!
>
> Costume drama aficionados will love the 2006 film adaptation of *The Painted Veil*, starring Naomi Watts as Kitty, Edward Norton as Walter, and Liev Schreiber as Charles. Not only are the costumes and sets simply exquisite, but so is the acting: Watts makes for a wonderfully impatient Kitty, Norton a very private but pained Walter, and Schreiber a deliciously slippery Charles.

Stuck in the hinterlands of 1920s China, in the midst of a cholera epidemic no less, Kitty wallows deep enough to make a modern reader want to airdrop her a twenty-first-century package of heartbreak helpers: a good bottle of wine, some quality chocolate, a pair of sweats, an iPod, and a few seasons of *Downton Abbey*. For days she sits at home ruminating over caddish Charles. Finally she makes a new friend and finds work at a local orphanage. Sure enough, before long she sees her former lover in a new light: "Charlie was stupid and vain, hungry for flattery, and she remembered the complacency with which he had told her little stories to prove his cleverness. He was proud of a low cunning. . . . The way he had treated her should have opened her eyes."

Only once you've suffered and studied your own pain can you acknowledge the red flags that fluttered before you all along, and as Kitty demonstrates, only with time can "What did I do wrong?" and "What could I have done differently?" become "What will I never do again?" Kitty's victory is a timeless one: Glorious is the moment when you realize you've come out on the other side not just wiser but a better, more caring person overall.

Rebecca West and the Old Maid

Among the many genius women writers of the twentieth century, Dame Rebecca West was arguably queen bee. Originally trained as an actress and without a formal education beyond age sixteen, West was one of the greatest public intellectuals of her time. As early as 1916, when she was just twenty-four, George Bernard Shaw noted that she "could handle a pen as brilliantly as ever I could and much more savagely." In 1947, *Time* called her "indisputably the world's number one woman writer"; a year later, when she received an award from President Harry Truman, he called her "the world's best reporter"—nice accolades for a woman who was still midcareer at the time. When she died at the accomplished old age of ninety-one, William Shawn, then the editor of the *New Yorker*, said that she was "one of the giants and will always have a lasting place in English literature. No one in this century wrote more dazzling prose, or had more wit, or looked at the intricacies of human character and the ways of the world more intelligently." Over the course of her career, she wrote at least ten works of fiction and nonfiction, covering whatever she pleased: the Nuremberg Trials, St. Augustine, Henry James, the last year of Queen Victoria's reign, Kafka, Balkan history and ethnography,

Hamlet, the significance of Nazism, suffragists, apartheid, and James Joyce's *Ulysses.* If ever a pen was mightier than the sword, it was hers.

It is therefore gratifying to see the human side of the genius, as illustrated in the following intimate letter. Her writing is potent but choppy, as if her usual glinting perfection was dulled by rage:

> During the next few days I shall either put a bullet through my head or commit something more shattering to myself than death. At any rate I shall be quite a different person. I refuse to be cheated out of my deathbed scene. I don't understand why you wanted me three months ago and don't want me now. . . . It's something I can't understand, something I despise. . . . I always knew that you would hurt me to death someday, but I hoped to choose the time and place. . . . You want a world of people falling over each other like puppies, people to quarrel and play with, people who rage and ache instead of people who burn. You can't conceive a person resenting the humiliation of an emotional failure so much that they twice tried to kill themselves: that seems silly to you. I can't conceive of a person who runs about lighting bonfires and yet nourishes a dislike of flame: that seems silly to me. You've literally ruined me.

Now, this might sound like a post-breakup letter, but the astonishing thing is that despite its raw ire, it did not in reality mark a finale. West wrote it when she was twenty-one, and not at the end of a relationship but rather at what proved to be the relative beginning—just a few months into what turned out to be a lengthy affair with a married man twenty-five years her senior. And that man was the author of *The Time Machine*, *The War of the Worlds*, and *The Invisible Man*, a literary titan of the sci-fi stripe, H. G. Wells.

According to Carl Rollyson's book *Rebecca West: A Life*, West and Wells first met around 1912 after she published a downright scornful review of his novel *Marriage*. "Mr. Wells's mannerisms are more infuriating than ever in *Marriage*," she wrote, adding the emasculating statement that he was "the old maid among novelists" and "even the sex obsession that lay clotted on [his earlier novels] like cold white sauce was merely old maid's mania, the reaction toward the flesh of a mind too long absorbed in airships and colloids."

No doubt determined to prove to her that he was anything but an "old maid," Wells invited her to lunch. Much to her shock, West discovered that he was "one of the most interesting men I have ever met." Within a couple of years, they became lovers (their erotic nicknames for each other were "Panther" (West) and "Jaguar" (Wells), and shortly after that—and after she drafted the letter quoted at length above—West found herself pregnant.

At the end of her pregnancy, Wells put her journalistic work on the back burner and wrote her first book, a critical study of Henry James. When it was published several years later, her enfant terrible approach horrified her fellow literary critics: James had died only a few months earlier, and they were astonished that the twenty-three-year-old had the audacity to criticize the literary giant's depictions of women.

Wells was at this point nearly twenty years into his second marriage, a union in which his taste for other (often much younger) women was tolerated. The West-Wells affair continued for another ten years. Their son, Anthony, later maintained that his childhood was marked by parental negligence, at least on his mother's part; in his fictionalized autobiography, *Heritage*, he revealed that until he was about five years old, his mother had demanded that he call her "Auntie" and his father "Wellsie" and that she dumped him in institutions during her numerous trips to the United States. (West countered that she was a working mother and those were the breaks for kids with working mothers. She saw to it that the book was never published in England. Needless to say, West and her son were never close.)

West initiated the breakup in 1923 after she spent years trying to persuade Wells to divorce his wife and marry her. His wife died in 1927, and not long afterward and five years after their split, West circled back to her initial scathing criticism of her lover in a particularly curious way, given that she'd had an affair and a child with him. In *The Strange Necessity: Essays and Reviews* (1928), West wrote that "all our youth they hung about the houses of our minds like Uncles, the Big Four: H. G. Wells, George Bernard Shaw, John Galsworthy, and Arnold Bennett." While Shaw playfully responded by sending her a postcard signed "your too affectionate uncle" and Bennett crafted and published a retort called "My Brilliant but Bewildering 'Niece,' " Wells was understandably offended. Surely he felt keenly that West's habit of distancing herself from her closest relationships with terms like "Auntie" and "Uncle"—the latter publicly—was just plain cruel.

Both Wells and West were listed, on the same page no less, of a Nazi document called *Sonderfahndungsliste G.B.* (translated literally as the Special Search List G.B. [Great Britain]), which named all the prominent British who were to be immediately arrested should the German invasion of Britain be successful. After the Allied victory, the compilation was found and christened "The Black Book," and those listed included not just obvious candidates like Winston Churchill but intellectuals and artists of all types, including E. M. Forster, Aldous Huxley, Bertrand Russell, Virginia Woolf, and Sigmund Freud. The majority of those listed were slated to be handed to the Gestapo. When Rebecca West heard about the list, she reportedly sent a telegram to the homosexual playwright and composer Noël Coward that said, "My dear—the people we should have been seen dead with."

Never Let Me Go

Lᴜʀᴋɪɴɢ ᴀᴛ ᴛʜᴇ heart of the technological revolution we've witnessed in recent decades is this question: How has it changed humanity? As any ethicist will tell you, with progress come moral tests, ones in which too often the fundamental rights of life, liberty, and happiness for all humans are put at risk. In short, we really have to worry when progress threatens values we hold dear, including those associated with our closest, most loving relationships.

Revealing the secrets of Kazuo Ishiguro's *Never Let Me Go* to those who have not yet read it or seen the film adaptation would be criminal. As a cautionary tale, it is that disquieting, complex, and important. Suffice it to say that it's in part a love triangle whose sharp corners are observant Kathy, angry Tommy, and brittle, manipulative Ruth, who grow up together in an English boarding school that shuffles the notion of elitism. At Hailsham there is comfort and even some joy, but every student is an underdog in Ishiguro's grand dystopian scheme of things.

If you can let go of the horror of the story itself and think of *Never Let Me Go* as a fable, then perhaps its point is not so unlike that of *The Velveteen Rabbit:* Love makes you real, or at least it should. On another level it illuminates the conditions and nature of forgiveness, which of course is a crucial if tender spot in matters of love, and on yet another level, through the clipped life spans of its characters, it explores the raison d'être of art, as well as that of love: Why bother if we're all going to die anyway?

But most important to our surroundings and where our society is blindly headed is the novel's probing at the underbelly of "progress"—what does it mean for love? We've seen it in our lifetimes: Technology and advances in the name of efficiency have already altered our understanding of what is okay in terms of love and kindness, whether it's the acceptability of dumping someone by text message or the mass clamor to explain the mysteries of love in terms of the excitable nature of neurons.

Of course scientific advances are wonderful, but slinking behind the gallop of each one is the prospect of its silently overtaking or even obliterating our moral imperatives, including the right to love and be loved.

♥ Film Alert!

Never Let Me Go was first published in 2005 and adapted to film in 2010, starring Carey Mulligan, Andrew Garfield, and Keira Knightley. The film version is utterly gorgeous, the acting is exquisite, and it perfectly captures the introspective nature of the book. But don't watch it alone, and don't watch it if you're depressed.

Hemingway and Wives

I F   Y O U ' R E   T H E   spouse of a writer, there's one cardinal commandment: *Thou shalt not lose the manuscripts.* And if there's one moment in literary history that can make you sweat sympathy bullets, it's the one when Hadley Richardson, Hemingway's first wife, realized that she'd done just that. As her train lurched out of Paris, she looked frantically around her stateroom only to conclude that the valise into which she'd stuffed all her husband's manuscripts had never made it from the platform. Later how she must have wondered if that momentary yet monumental lapse in her perfectionism was the first crack in their marriage.

According to *The Hemingway Women*, by Bernice Kert, one of the many investigations into Hemingway's infamous love life, when Hadley reached Lausanne, where her husband met her at the station, she was in such hysterics she couldn't tell him what had happened. He reassured her that no matter what it was that had happened, it couldn't possibly be *that* bad. When she finally did manage to get the truth out, he kept his cool, which was actually worse than if he'd fallen into a rage. "Part of the horror of the experience was watching him gamely pretend that it didn't matter," Kert writes. "She watched numbly as he boarded the day train for Paris. He needed to see for himself that everything was lost."

Two stories survived the loss of the valise—one was tucked away in a bureau drawer, and the other was being read by editors in New York— but everything else, including fragments of a novel and sketches of life in Paris, was gone. Ezra Pound suggested that if the work was good, Hemingway could reconstruct it, while his friends Gertrude Stein and Alice B. Toklas tried to distract him with nice lunches. But Ernest never really got over the loss, and decades later, long after their marriage had ended, mere mention of the incident made Hadley shiver.

From Hadley to Pauline . . .

Four years later, when Pauline Pfeiffer entered the scene and pro-ceeded to set her sights on breaking up Hadley and Ernest's mar-riage, surely "part of the horror" for Hadley was watching her husband yet again "gamely pretend that it didn't matter." Pauline was a chic rich girl who worked for *Vogue* and was a player in the Parisian expat scene; Hadley was eight years older than Heming-way and after bearing their child, Bumby, was looking more dumpy than posh.

Pauline entered their circle just as Hemingway was finishing *The Torrents of Spring*, a novella that satirized the pretensions of writers and took particular aim at Sherwood Anderson. Problem was, Sherwood was an old friend of Hadley and Ernest from their Chicago days—indeed the friend who convinced them to move to Paris—and Hadley thought *Torrents of Spring* was a cruel and nasty betrayal. Hemingway's friend John Dos Passos took the mid-dle road and found the book funny but thought it shouldn't be published. Ever the strategist, though, Pauline found it uproari-ously funny and urged him to publish it.

♥ Dirty Pool

When it came to dirty pool, Hemingway was a shark. He wrote *The Torrents of Spring* in ten days, intending it not only as a spoof of American literati but also as a way to force a break with his publisher, Boni and Liveright. Hemingway's contract stipulated that he was to publish his next three works with Boni and Liveright, but if they rejected any work he submitted to them, the contract could be terminated. With the submission of *Torrents of Spring*, Boni and Liveright were forced into a corner: They had to turn it down because Sherwood Anderson was their author. Hemingway was then free to move on to the more prestigious Scribners, which published the novella and all his subsequent work.

While she was terribly supportive of her husband's work, Hadley was a no-nonsense type, and when Pauline showered Hemingway with endless flattery, it caught his attention. She pulled out all the stops when it came to insinuating herself, including spending Christmas of 1925 with the Hemingways in Austria, where her flirtation with Ernest intensified when he taught her how to ski. (Ah, the age-old ploy of the bunny slope!) Pauline's duplicity was by any measure stunning. Even as she seduced Hemingway, she wrote Hadley letters including doozy lines like "I've missed you simply *indecently*" and begged her to come back to Paris.

By February 1926, Ernest and Pauline were likely having an affair. He was on a high after completing *The Sun Also Rises* and placing it with a new publisher, and she was on the high of knowing that her conniving was paying off. Hadley surely suspected but hoped that whatever was going on would pass. According to Kert, when Hadley, Pauline, and Pauline's sister, Jinny, took a trip to the Loire Valley that spring and Pauline was bitchy to Hadley, Hadley asked Jinny if Pauline was in love with Ernest. Jinny conceded that yes, the two were fond of each other. Jinny did not reveal, however, just how determined her sister was to relieve Ernest of his plain, boring wife.

When Hadley confronted Ernest, he not only denied the liaison but, in a classically manipulative move, turned it around and put her in the wrong for bringing it up. In an outstanding feat of acquiescence, Hadley allowed Pauline to join her and Ernest on a vacation on the Côte d'Azur. "Here it was," Hadley remembered years later, "that the three breakfast trays, three wet bathing suits on the line, three bicycles were to be found. Pauline tried to teach me to dive, but I was not a success." It wouldn't have been a surprise if Pauline had tried to teach Hadley to dive in shallow water.

Hadley and Ernest split up shortly thereafter, and Ernest and Pauline moved in together in Paris. Hadley then offered Ernest a deal: If Ernest and Pauline stayed apart for a hundred days and still wanted to be together, she would grant him a divorce. For the cooling-off period, Hadley decamped to the States, where she was miserable and wrote Ernest letters that included lines like "We are one, we are the same guy, I am you," while her very Catholic mother gave her the silent treatment.

Back in Paris, Hadley asked Ernest to take care of Bumby while she took a few days to reflect on the situation. On November 26, 1926, short of the hundred days, she informed Ernest of her decision: She was ready for a divorce. When he promised her the royalties from *The Sun Also Rises*, she thanked him and encouraged him to maintain his relationship with their son, and when she wrote him letters covering the logistics of their split, she signed them as she had in happier times, with "Mummy's love." And when he hired a cart to move her possessions into her new apartment and burst into tears, she appeared unmoved.

. . . and Pauline to Martha . . .

Five months after his divorce was finalized, Ernest married Pauline, and together the two left for Key West. Three sons, eleven years, and *A Farewell to Arms* later, a group of tourists walked into a bar, Sloppy Joe's, which Hemingway frequented. Among them was a girl with golden hair and wearing a black cotton dress. Ernest returned the next evening, hoping she'd be there again. He didn't make it home for the dinner party Pauline had planned for that night.

While Hadley and Pauline were no slouches intellectually, in Martha Gellhorn, who was twenty-eight in 1936, Hemingway had met his match in terms of ambition. Like Hadley she had gone to Bryn Mawr, but unlike Hadley she'd aggressively pursued a career as a writer. And like Pauline she had once worked in the Paris office of *Vogue*, but unlike Pauline she'd gone on to publish short stories in the *New Yorker* and *Harper's Bazaar* and had written a successful book about poverty in America. Unlike both of them, she didn't have catering to a man in her DNA.

After meeting Martha, who went by the sportier "Marty," Ernest took off for Spain to cover the Spanish Civil War and insisted that Pauline could not join him. Shortly thereafter Marty met up with him in Madrid, which had by that point been under siege for four months. In a scenario that's nearly cliché for illicit couplings among war correspondents, Marty and Ernest were outed when a shell hit their hotel at night, forcing couples from their bedrooms.

Soon Marty was a correspondent for *Collier's*, a prominent leftist weekly in the States, and together she and Ernest were going to and from the front (which in Madrid during the Civil War was often just a few blocks away) in an armored car. "All her life

Martha remained grateful to Ernest for teaching her about the different sounds of gunfire and when to fall flat," writes Bernice Kert. And while Marty maintained that their sexual chemistry was never all that, any journalist knows that there's nothing hotter than falling in love in a war zone.

Marty and Ernest made multiple trips to Spain to cover the war, and in Madrid it was an open secret that they were lovers. By 1939 he and Pauline were estranged, and in 1940 he and Martha were married three weeks after his divorce was finalized.

But being married to Hemingway was different from being his mistress. Marty was accustomed to covering the world's hot spots—those inflamed by the events leading up to World War II, like Finland under siege by the Soviets and Central Europe during the rise of Hitler—with freedom and top-notch aplomb, while Hemingway was accustomed to women who bowed to him, didn't have a temper as violent as his, and, perhaps more important, weren't his equal as writers. When she was reporting from the Italian front in the spring of 1944, Ernest thundered by cable, ARE YOU A WAR CORRESPONDENT OR WIFE IN MY BED?

If the cardinal commandment for spouses of writers is *Thou shalt not lose the manuscripts*, then the cardinal one for married journalists is *Thou shalt not steal thy spouse's job*. In April 1944 Ernest offered his services to *Collier's*, Marty's employer for seven years by that point, knowing that the magazine could have only one front-line correspondent and fully aware of the fact that as Ernest Hemingway he had every American magazine—not just *Collier's*—at his beck and call.

As if that weren't nasty enough, when he subsequently got a seat on an official plane transporting journalists and entertainers from America to Europe and Marty asked if he could maybe help her get a seat, too, he said, "Oh, no. I couldn't do that. They only fly men," when in fact plenty of women were booked. According to Bernice

Kert, Marty's only way to the European arena then was as the sole passenger aboard a freighter loaded with dynamite but no lifeboats.

When she finally arrived in London weeks after him, Ernest was in a hospital with a concussion, a retinue, and champagne and whiskey bottles under the bed. This was not appropriate behavior in time of war, Marty thought, so she walked out on him. Forever, as it turned out.

Marty had her revenge, Gellhorn style, shortly thereafter on D-Day. Given his stature, Ernest learned about the invasion a few days ahead of time and was sent to a secret staging area. She, however, only learned about it at a morning briefing a few hours into the action. She hustled down to the port, sneaked on board a hospital ship that would sail at dawn, and locked herself in a toilet. On the night of June 7, she managed to get ashore by impersonating a stretcher bearer. Ernest never got any farther than the bridge of the landing craft.

> To this day Martha Gellhorn is remembered for her phenomenal war reportage. "I followed the war wherever I could reach it," she once said. She was among the few journalists on the scene when the Dachau concentration camp was liberated. "Behind the barbed wire and the electric fence the skeletons sat in the sun and searched themselves for lice. They have no age and no faces; they all look alike and like nothing you will ever see, if you are lucky," she wrote.

. . . and Then Martha to Mary

In 1946, Ernest married *Time* magazine correspondent Mary Welsh, whom he'd met just before he was hospitalized in London and to whom proposed the third time they encountered each other. (Mary later recalled that the first time they met, he said, "I don't know you, Mary. But I want to marry you. . . . You're beautiful, like a May fly." Together they traveled all over Europe and then took on Africa, where they survived two plane crashes in two days. (In the first the plane crash-landed after meeting with a utility pole, leaving Ernest with a head wound and Mary with broken ribs; in the second their plane exploded at takeoff, and Ernest walked away with another concussion and burns.) Soon he was burned in yet another accident, a bush fire, and only months later did a doctor's tally in Europe fully capture the extent of his injuries: Both his liver and a kidney were ruptured, he had two cracked disks and a dislocated shoulder, not to mention a fractured skull.

You probably know how the story winds up from there: Mary was Ernest's caretaker through his long, boozy decline, sticking with him through thick and thin, including when he smashed her typewriter and when he started an affair with a nineteen-year-old.

Hadley and Ernest remained amicable, and she enjoyed a second marriage to Paul Mowrer, a Pulitzer Prize–winning journalist. Pauline never married again. Martha Gellhorn had numerous affairs and then married *Time* magazine's managing editor in 1954 and divorced him in 1963. By her own admission, sex was never her thing; she once noted, "I daresay I was the worst bed partner in five continents." Of her marriage to Hemingway, she wrote, "I weep for the eight years I spent . . . worshipping his image with him, and I weep for whatever else I was cheated of due to that time-serving."

In the end one has to wonder if Hemingway's ex-wives read his work, knowing that they'd likely recognize shards of their respective marriages to him in it. At any rate, it's gratifying to know that Hadley lived until 1979 and Martha until 1998—both long enough to derive some gratification out of seeing their ex put on trial for misogyny in the court of public opinion.

Eternal Question of Eternal Sunshine

IF THE WORLD were entitled to only one breakup movie, *Eternal Sunshine of the Spotless Mind* would be it—nothing else is smarter, more thought-provoking, better crafted, better cast, or just plain beautiful. Its portrayal of the fabulousness of falling in love and the horror of its falling apart is genius unadulterated.

Kate Winslet and Jim Carrey play Clementine and Joel, a couple whose relationship has gone nastily south. Both elect to submit to a procedure that erases their memories of the other. Winslet is pitch-perfect (as always), this time embodying Clem, who from one moment to the next is a charming eccentric, a volatile bully, or an attentive girlfriend, while Jim Carrey (minus the creepy smile he relies on in comedy) plays the quiet, introspective Joel. And whether they are in a scene together, like when an arm-in-arm stroll through a flea market suddenly erupts into a knock-down-drag-out, or alone, like when Joel, in his car, drives away from Clementine, tears streaming down his face, both are spellbinding.

Much as we might not identify with the specifics of the characters (Clementine dyes her hair electric blue and tangerine, and Joel is almost obnoxiously passive), the universality of what they experience during their breakup will resonate with anyone who has really been through the wringer—namely, the bargaining. What would you do to make the pain of heartbreak go away? Given the opportunity, would you trade all your memories of a relationship for peace? The film forces you to do the calculus of what if: If you could delete all the bad memories (the fights, the recriminations, the heartbreak of the aftermath), but if doing so demanded that you delete the good ones, too (good-bye first kiss, sex for hours, and the oxytocin high of moments that only the two of you shared), would you do it? Tough call, but probably one with which most of us would err on the side of caution. It is better to have loved and lost and remember it than to not remember it at all.

Eternal Sunshine also forces its audience to make a private inventory of the items they've held on to—the memory triggers of past relationships—and to deconstruct, if they were to have all memories erased, what items they'd need to take to a Dr. Mierzwiak. For example, you might be able to expunge all the items from your home that remind you of an ex, but what about the things outside your home that send you down memory lane? Like the phenomenon of what I call déjà vroom (or alternatively déjà gloom), when you see a car that is exactly like your ex's and before you know it, you've swiveled around to see if it's him?

One of my favorite scenes in *Eternal Sunshine* is when Joel is unconscious on his pullout couch, deep in the procedure that is erasing his memories of Clem, while two other characters, Mary and Stan, are stoned, jumping on the mattress in their undies, on either side of him. No scene captures better what I think is the supreme irony of heartbreak: that it is universal and yet profoundly isolating. When you're in the throes of heartbreak, it is as if everyone around you is partying in their panties.

A handful of the best lines from *Eternal Sunshine*:

Joel: "Random thoughts for Valentine's Day 2004. Today is a holiday invented by greeting card companies to make people feel like crap."

Clementine: "Maybe you can find yourself a nice antique rocking chair to die in."

Joel: "Are we like couples you see in restaurants? Are we the dining dead?"

Mary: "No, I'm sorry Mrs. Timmon. You can't have the procedure done three times in one night. . . . Well, it's just not our policy here."

Joel: "Is there any risk of brain damage?"

Dr. Mierzwiak: "Well, technically speaking, the procedure is brain damage, but it's on a par with a night of heavy drinking."

"Eternal sunshine of the spotless mind" is a line from "Eloisa to Abelard," a poem by Alexander Pope that plays on the story of Heloise and Abelard (see p. 9) and envisions Heloise begging to forget the entire relationship.

> How happy is the blameless vestal's lot!
> The world forgetting, by the world forgot.
> Eternal sunshine of the spotless mind!
> . . .
> No, fly me, fly me, far as pole from pole;
> Rise Alps between us! and whole oceans roll!
> Ah, come not, write not, think not once of me,
> Nor share one pang of all I felt for thee.
> Thy oaths I quit, thy memory resign;
> Forget, renounce me, hate whate'er was mine.

Misogyny, Thy Name Is Norman Mailer

Norman Mailer booty-called Adele Morales, the woman who would become his second wife, before he had even met her. It was 2:00 AM in the spring of 1951, shortly after Norman had separated from his wife, Beatrice Silverman, and he had been up drinking with his friend Dan Wolf. Dan suggested that they give his good-looking friend Adele a call, thinking that Norman would enjoy her company. At first Adele demurred when she was roused in the middle of the night. But when Norman offered to pay the fare for a cab ride from her apartment in Greenwich Village up to East Sixty-fourth Street and then quoted F. Scott Fitzgerald, she agreed, likely donned an item from her reputedly vast collection of Frederick's of Hollywood lingerie, and hailed a cab. As Mary Dearborn describes in *Mailer: A Biography*, within hours they were lovers, within days they were living in adjoining apartments, and within weeks Norman was knocking down the walls in said apartments to make one out of the two.

While Beatrice was mellow and Jewish, Adele was the classic fiery Latina. She apparently layered Gypsy-like attire over her lingerie, was of Spanish and Peruvian descent, and, most appealingly to Norman, had slept with a famous man: Jack Kerouac. Norman and Adele's sexual connection was electric, and Norman took pride in her orgasmic abilities (multiples were apparently her norm). They both thrived on drama, whether it was a lesbian encounter or a little game she played at parties in which she'd tell Norman that she'd slept with one of the male guests but not which one, driving him to the point of complete distraction.

Adele hadn't been much into substance abuse when she first met Norman, but under his tutelage she took up liquor, pot, and prescription drugs, and by the summer of 1954, the year they got married, both were well known for their hard-partying ways. They cleaned up long enough to have a baby girl, Danielle, in 1957, and moved to Connecticut. By this time it was apparently one thing for Adele to sleep with women but quite another for anyone to gossip about it. When Norman's friend William Styron allegedly had the audacity to share with someone the fact that Adele swung both ways, Norman dropped him a line that was classic Mailer mean: "So I tell you this, Billy-boy. You have got to learn to keep your mouth shut about my wife, for if you do not, and I hear of it again, I will invite you to a fight in which I expect to stomp out of you a fat amount of your yellow and treacherous shit." By 1958, back in New York, Adele and Norman regularly ended their wild nights by going home with other people. At parties hosted by George Plimpton, editor of the *Paris Review*, Norman was known for having drunken staring matches with gorgeous women.

In more ways than one, 1960 proved to be a banner year for Norman. He got his big break covering politics by writing about the Democratic National Convention for *Esquire* (no small feat given that even by his own admission he had no political connections whatsoever), publishing "Superman Comes to the Supermarket"—now regarded as one of the great classics of New Journalism—right around the same time an account of his drunken antics in Provincetown was published in the *New Yorker*, giving Mailer watchers plenty to chew on. As Dearborn tells it, then he decided to run in the New York mayoral race, thinking that he'd have a solid constituency in the city's prostitutes, runaways, hipsters, and criminals, and he hit his own sister in the face when she produced campaign materials that displeased him. Then one night at a lecture at Brown University, he made an obscene gesture to a student and subsequently began rambling about knives. His friends were understandably flummoxed—nasty Norman was the norm, but even for him this was worrisome behavior. As his biographer Mary Dearborn wisely observes, "It is a curious phenomenon of celebrity that people will watch in grim fascination when a certain kind of public figure seems to be running amok."

But all hell broke loose the night of November 19, at a party at the Mailers' apartment that was intended to be an unofficial kick-off for his mayoral campaign and that, astonishingly, their two young children were home for. Dressed in a bullfighter's shirt, Norman presided over a gathering that was surreal from the start. He invited strangers and homeless people in from the street, and a scuffle broke out between Allen Ginsberg and another writer, Norman Podhoretz, who had just published an unflattering piece about the Beats called "The Know-Nothing Bohemians." Norman struck George Plimpton in the face with a rolled-up newspaper because George hadn't brought enough power brokers to the event, and the two came to blows. Adele locked herself in the bathroom, and Norman challenged Random House editor Jason Epstein to a boxing match. At 3:00 AM, when only about twenty people were left of the some three hundred who had been there a few hours earlier, Norman forced them to divide themselves into two lines: one for his friends and one for his enemies. The former included their Jamaican maid, and the latter may or may not have included Adele. Within a few minutes, he was down on the street.

At around 4:30 AM, Norman returned to the apartment and

appeared to have been in a street fight, complete with a black eye. Then, goaded by a taunt from Adele, who had by this time emerged from the bathroom, he stabbed her in the chest with a filthy two-and-a-half-inch-long penknife, penetrating her breast and narrowly missing her heart.

What happened after that is, of course, a bit foggy. Norman appears to have passed out and then disappeared for a few hours, and at the hospital Adele underwent lengthy emergency surgery and was found to have a pierced cardiac sac. She told her doctors that she had fallen on some glass. A few days later, Norman pulled off an interview with the famously aggressive Mike Wallace, who knew nothing of the stabbing, as if he were sane. But within a few days after that, Norman was involuntarily committed to Bellevue, where he spent seventeen days.

Ultimately Adele did admit that her husband had stabbed her, but she refused to press charges. He was indicted by a grand jury after his release from Bellevue, and he pleaded guilty and was put on probation for three years. He never publicly expressed remorse over the incident and many years later told the *New York Times* that "a decade's anger made me do it. After that, I felt better."

Amazingly, Adele and Norman struggled along for another year or so. Adele later wrote, "I told myself that if he were still dangerous, he would still be in the hospital. . . . Whatever else happened, I knew in my heart that Norman would never physically harm [the girls]. As for me, what more could he do that he hadn't done?"

So the saying goes, denial ain't just a river in Egypt.

Finally a quickie divorce granted in Mexico in April 1962 ended the Norman-Adele drama duo once and for all. That same year, he published a book of poetry called *Deaths for the Ladies (and Other Disasters)*, that included a poem called "Rainy Afternoon with the Wife" that implied that the stabbing was an act of love.

Next Stop: Aristocracy

Free of Adele, Norman wasted little time moving on to Lady Jeanne Campbell, whom he had met a few months earlier at Gore Vidal's Christmas party.

Lady Jeanne was quite the man-eater, and like her parents, she was "colorful." Her playboy father, heir to the dukedom of Argyll, was a gambling addict who took his bride, daughter of a newspaper magnate, to a brothel in order for her to observe firsthand her marital duties. Their union lasted just a year and a half, until, at least according to Jeanne's obituary in the British newspaper *The Telegraph*, casinos and an American girl called "Oui Oui" proved particularly attractive to her father.

After Jeanne began a clandestine affair with Sir Oswald Mosley, a near-geriatric baronet who also happened to be England's leading fascist, her powerful grandfather, Lord Beaverbrook, packed her off to New York to write for one of his own papers, the *London Evening Standard*. Within a few years, she'd landed a job at *Time* and took up with the married Henry Luce II, Time-Life's owner and founder. She was still with "Harry" Luce when she met Norman, to whom she was attracted, she later told Gore Vidal, because she "had never gone to bed with a Jew before." As for Norman, while some of the draw lay in Jeanne's buxom vivacity, the unfamiliar but luscious territory presented by her aristocratic background and the fact that she'd bedded Harry Luce, whom he hated as the embodiment of "the Establishment," were points in her favor. As Mary Dearborn writes, "With Jeanne, he was not merely inheriting the mistress of one of the most powerful men in publishing. He was also getting revenge."

Within a year of their first meeting, Jeanne was pregnant. They married in secret but went on a honeymoon to Europe to meet her grandfather, after which Lord Beaverbrook decreased her inheritance by $10 million. (It has to be said, one can only imagine how distressed any man would be to see his progeny bring home a man like Norman Mailer.) Their daughter—Mailer's fourth—was born in August of 1962, but a year later their relationship was already on the rocks. Norman enjoyed bragging to his friends that his wife had given up $10 million for him, and, as Dearborn points out, Jeanne didn't prove to be like Adele at all—she wasn't game to wear an apron, pour him another drink, and plan another party. Moreover, she didn't rise to his many baits. Jeanne left him for good in January 1963, and on his fortieth birthday, a few days later, he propositioned Gloria Steinem (who turned him down but did him the honor of remaining his friend). Several years later he told an interviewer, "I like to marry women whom I can beat once in a while, and who fight back." He later repurposed Jeanne as the ultimate bitch in his novel *An American Dream*, still later tipping his hat to her with the admission that she was a "dear pudding of a lady" and as "interesting" and "Machiavellian" as he himself was.

Giving Henry VIII a Run for His Money

Norman's marriages four, five, and six proved dramatic in their own unsurprising ways. Between 1963 and 1980, he was married to Beverly Bentley, a model/actress, whom he beat and taunted with his affairs. From there he moved on to Carol Stevens, a jazz singer whom he married one day and divorced the next in 1980, in order to make their daughter, who had been born nine years earlier, legitimate. He married his last wife, the model Norris Church, in 1980, five years after she sent him a love poem and he returned it to her, marked up with his criticisms, and two years after they had a son together. In her memoir, which she published three years after Norman's death in 2007, she wrote, "Well, I bought a ticket to the circus. I don't know why I was surprised to see elephants."

But when it comes to the six wives of Norman Mailer, the best-revenge award goes to Lady Jeanne: She was rumored to have moved right on from Norman to have affairs with President John F. Kennedy, Nikita Khrushchev, and Fidel Castro, all between October 1963 and May 1964. (The dalliance with Kennedy reportedly occurred in her Georgetown house the month before he was assassinated, the one with Khrushchev at his dacha in April 1964, and then the next month she allegedly moved on to Castro in Havana.) Later she married a massively wealthy heir to railway fortunes, John Sergeant Cram III, presumably in part to recoup the $10 million she lost on account of Norman. She had a second daughter, Cusi, during her brief marriage to Cram, who wasn't his but reportedly fathered by the Bolivian ambassador. Rumor has it that when she received a huge advance to write her memoirs, she blew it on a villa in Greece. At the end of her life, she lived quietly in a walk-up in Greenwich Village, where she slept in one of her few enduring acquisitions: a collapsible campaign bed that had belonged to Napoleon.

Closer

FIRST, a note of caution: If you've been through a breakup that featured infidelity, settle in for the night with a different film, unless you need reassurance that the demise of your relationship didn't plumb the very depths of cruelty, because that's exactly what *Closer*'s characters do. To perfection.

The film-review cliché "not for the emotionally squeamish" appears to have been coined in response to *Closer,* a play written by Patrick Marber in 1997 and adapted for film by Mike Nichols in 2004. It's basically an excruciating string of confrontations, issued through short, snappy dialogue. In the film it's hard to determine which scene is the most squeamworthy: When Anna photographs a crying Alice, knowing she's caused the tears? When Anna confesses just a few months into her marriage with Larry that she's been having an affair with Dan for over a year? When Dan reveals to Alice that he's been sleeping with Anna and she demands to know how deception actually works? Or when Alice strips for Larry and says, "Lying is the most fun a girl can have without taking her clothes off, but it's better if you do"?

Against the backdrop of a dark, shiny, and chic London, *Closer* poses the macro questions that really lie at the heart of any intimate relationship: Does sharing the truth, the whole truth, and nothing but the truth honor those you love? What exactly are the perimeters of the gray area where some infidelity is forgivable? And what are the ingredients that make an infidelity solidly, irrevocably unforgivable?

The stars of the film version are all such astonishingly attractive and charismatic people (Julia Roberts, Clive Owen, Jude Law, and Natalie Portman, each of whom is riveting) that I think it also poses a question that in today's Photoshopped, perfection-obsessed culture is highly relevant: Are beautiful people inherently more selfish? A 2011 study by Spanish researchers indicated that yes, they are. The more symmetrical a person's face is (perfect example: Natalie Portman), the more likely he or she is to be perceived as beautiful by others, and this correlates with a less cooperative personality. If that is the case, then I think with *Closer* a key question for audience members becomes this: As observers, do we give physically beautiful people more leeway or less when it comes to duplicitous behavior? To put it another way, if the characters in *Closer* were more ordinary-looking, would we sympathize with them more or less? In *Closer* everyone is gorgeous, everyone is bad, and even the most sympathetic character, Alice, shows them all up in a stunning last-minute reveal.

Moving past the great-beauty question, for us mere mortals one of *Closer*'s more relevant questions is about ex sex. Given the choice, would you want to know or not know that your last act of intimacy with a loved one is indeed the last? Would you want to remember it as the usual—or perhaps not remember it at all just because it was so usual—or remember it as an emotion-packed grand finale? With one last act of love, can you lay the first stone in the worthwhile monument to your loss, or is it the stupidest thing you can possibly do?

♥ Film Alert!

Another great film about love and cruelty is *Dangerous Liaisons* (1988), starring Glenn Close, John Malkovich, Michelle Pfeiffer, and Uma Thurman. In it, two aristocrats, the vicomte de Valmont (Malkovich) and the marquise de Merteuil (Close) scheme to break hearts for the sheer thrill of it. At one point Valmont says to the marquise, "I thought 'betrayal' was your favorite word," to which the marquise replies, "No, no . . . 'cruelty.' I always think that has a nobler ring to it."

High Fidelity

Rare is the film that in terms of quality matches the book that inspired it, but *High Fidelity* pulls it off. The film version, from 2000, stars the eternally adorably John Cusack as a moderately feckless record-store owner whose girlfriend leaves him. Laugh-out-loud funny as the film is (like the book), it's also a thoughtful meditation on the various stimuli that are part and parcel to heartbreak, including music. In the first moments of the film, Rob wonders, "What came first, the music or the misery? People worry about kids playing with guns, or watching violent videos, that some sort of culture of violence will take them over. Nobody worries about kids listening to thousands, literally thousands, of songs about heartbreak, rejection, pain, misery, and loss. Did I listen to pop music because I was miserable? Or was I miserable because I listened to pop music?" Back to the age-old question: Is heartbreak made all the more keen because we have words, music, and art to express the pain?

But *High Fidelity* is also an intelligent and thorough rumination on what psychologists call the "primacy effect." When his girlfriend, Laura, leaves him because he can't really commit, Rob is compelled to inventory his "top five heartbreaks," starting with Alison Ashmore, the first girl he kissed and the first girl to ditch him way back in seventh grade. As he remembers that awful day on the track field, Rob says that "there seems to be an element of that afternoon in everything that's happened to me since. All my romantic stories are a scrambled version of that first one."

The primacy effect is the power of firsts. You know how you remember your first kiss, your first sip of beer, your first wobble down the road without training wheels, but not the second, sixth, or twentieth? Such is the power of the intensity and novelty of first experiences—they sear our brains in a way that later ones simply don't, and the glow from them lights the path to our deathbeds. A first love is incredibly powerful, imprinting an experience on our gray matter that gets reactivated in some fashion every subsequent time we experience love. It stands to reason, then, that the primacy effect activates with heartbreak—each time our heart gets broken, some part of our brain returns to that very first one, as well as others, to feel all the pain again, to reread all the messages. Over the years heartbreak becomes a palimpsest; consciously or not, you always revisit the pain that came before.

In the very last scene of the *High Fidelity*, after the inventory and the self-recrimination, Rob finally gets it together and decides that he is tired of being distracted by the fantasy of perfect love, of the heartbreak parade. "I'm just sick of thinking about it all the time," he says. "I want to think about something else." He commits to Laura, once and for all, and embraces moving on to other problems.

This is what I like to think of as heartbreak fatigue at its best. At a certain point, love gone wrong wears thin. Preoccupation with it becomes utterly self-defeating and terribly *old*. It becomes boring, and you become a bore. Perhaps more than at any other time in your life, once you reach this point, like Rob, the ball is in your court. Eventually one has to say, "Been there, done that," prop open the door to the familiar, and march right back to it.

· V ·

CONCLUSION AND
PRACTICAL ADVICE

I WAS ABLE TO write this book only once my heartbreak became history, confined to my own rearview mirror. Only when I had a loving husband and delightful son could I revisit the tiny personal horrors of being dumped by men I loved, or thought I loved, and try to jigger them into a larger scheme. I could write *The Little Book of Heartbreak* only once I felt in some measure safe from its subject matter.

This is not to say that going forward I'm invulnerable to having my heart smashed to pieces, and I have to admit that for the duration of working on this book a certain amount of nostalgia colored my research and my writing. Some days that took the form of digging up a photo of an ex or sneaking a listen to my favorite heartbreak songs in the car while taking my son to school, just to refresh my memory on how badly it sucks. Other days it meant thinking so hard about the many ironies that orbit heartbreak that my head hurt: that it's universal and yet profoundly lonely, that it makes you feel alive and dead, that wallowing in sadness makes you feel better. Even if memories of it are old and withered, heartbreak still makes us human.

At the close of what I hope is a poignant and informative waltz with the characters and creations of heartbreak, it would feel remiss of me to not offer any words of wisdom to those looking for them. So here you go, from one expert on heartbreak to another.

Diversions

Heloise threw herself into her work, Lusanna may have perfected her needlepoint, Mary Wollstonecraft traveled. Needless to say, finding worthwhile diversions is key, and while one should never discount the therapeutic benefits of drinking too much Maker's Mark and shagging someone new, here are a few diversionary tactics that might help quicken the transition from pain to wisdom:

- Read lots and lots of whatever makes you feel better, whether it's Nora Roberts novels, *The Lord of the Rings*, or one of the books I suggest. It's okay to read in bed in your pjs in the beginning, but shake it up eventually and read in a park or a café.
- Never underestimate the power of endorphins. Exercise. This is *not* when you should bail on going to the gym. Even if the last thing you want to do is leave the house, kickboxing in times of trouble does a body good. If ever there was a time when you need to feel less like the Pillsbury Doughgirl rather than more, this is it.
- Take a sledgehammer to your routines. Used to staying in town all weekend or going to the same farmers' market week after week? Then mix it up. Novelty is your new best friend.
- Never underestimate the power of a good laugh. Watch *Bridesmaids* if that does the trick, see a comedy show, sit in

your bed and stream *Little Britain* or *Arrested Development* on Netflix.

- Volunteering can put your own life in perspective. Work a few shifts in a soup kitchen or at the Humane Society. Don't let it make you sanctimonious, but really, helping a person who has no home or taking a happy three-legged dog for a walk can knock things back into their proper scale.

- Even if you're not a sex or a love addict, going to an open SLAA (Sex and Love Addicts Anonymous) meeting is almost as good as taking a happy three-legged dog for a walk. And you just might learn something useful.

On Wallowing

While of course taking wallowing to the Havisham extreme, or even that of Liszt when he made himself sick with disappointment as a young man, is dangerous business, it does have its place. Grief over the death of a relationship is in essence a long, excruciating, one-sided good-bye. It demands hunkering down, replaying the events again and again in your head while the pain in your chest overtakes all other physical sensations, tormenting yourself with visions of how things might have ended differently or, better yet, not ended at all. This is perfectly normal and in fact healthy, much as it might feel like the reverse.

When you're in a deep wallow, it's important to remind yourself (and anyone else who might be giving you a hard time about it) that many psychologists think that heartbreak—and wallowing—exists for very explicit reasons, the first of which is to teach us valuable lessons. As a psychologist I spoke to put it, "That pain is there to tell you something about relationships, about what kind of relationship is good for you. The pain makes sure that you focus on it so you learn. Don't rob yourself of the opportunity to learn. You need to *listen* to it." So maybe you learn not to hover, maybe you learn that men who love dogs more than they love women are bad news, maybe you learn never to date another perpetual student. Whatever the lesson is, without the pain of a breakup you wouldn't stop, focus, and absorb, even if it's on an unconscious level. In short, bad feelings are not necessarily a bad thing.

A second reason that heartbreak exists is that while on an existential level, it reminds us that ultimately we die alone, it also helps us reach out to others, thereby strengthening and even expanding the social networks we rely on to live. Attending book readings, drinking happy-hour sangria, and signing up for a class on whatever piques your interest—these all qualify as distractions but also fall under the rubric of "expanding your social network." The important thing is to emerge from the cave of heartbreak as a more caring individual, not a less caring one.

Get to Know Your Attachment Style

It's important to come to terms with the fact that people have very different capacities for intimacy (good examples of extremes might be Johannes Brahms, who struggled to express his feelings and to have intimate relationships, and Oskar Kokoschka, who wore his heart on his sleeve). And while I wouldn't want to get all self-helpy on you, being aware of where you fall in the spectrum of attachment, and where your partners seem to fall, can be helpful. Reading up on attachment styles is a good place to start. From there you might be able to piece together, on a very general yet still-instructive level, what to look for and what to avoid in the future.

Drugs

While some people may be more inclined to categorize drugs in terms of "legal" and "illegal," when it comes to heartbreak, the following delineations might be more helpful:

1. *Drugs that help treat a root problem.* For example, consider the case of someone whose serotonin levels are so low that she has a negative, repetitive thinking pattern that affects her ability to have a successful relationship. This is a situation where an SSRI, like Prozac or Zoloft, might stop a nasty pattern in its tracks.

2. *Drugs that help you get through the crisis.* If you're anxious about an impending event, like seeing an ex at a party (*Why does he still have to look so cute?*) or going through the excruciating exchange of personal belongings at a subway stop (*Here are your boxers and your iPod—I threw out your toothbrush*), welcoming Xanax or Ativan with a cheery smile might be just the thing. Antianxiety drugs like these can also help you get that much-needed good night's sleep, as can natural treatments like magnesium, 5-HTP, melatonin, or valerian.

3. *Drugs that help you digest the crisis.* At the risk of having the DEA storm my house, I'll venture that if sitting in the bathtub smoking a joint and listening to "When Doves Cry" on repeat helps you have a genuine, enduring eureka moment that really helps you get somewhere, then you should do it.

In short, if you're deep in the well of heartbreak and are a virgin when it comes to self-medication, in my humble, albeit experienced, opinion, there's no time like the present.

How Long Will It Take?

Some say for every year you're with someone, expect a month to feel better. Others use a more elastic formula: Getting over it takes half the amount of time as the relationship lasted, so if you were in the relationship for a year, then expect six months to get over it. Needless to say, I think recovery time is impossible to estimate, given all the variables, as we've seen: Franz Liszt appears to have gotten over his relationship with Marie d'Agoult more quickly than she did; for Joni Mitchell getting over Graham Nash took at least an extended vacation and however long it took to record *Blue*; and *The Painted Veil*'s Kitty sees the light regarding Charlie in a few short weeks. The fact is, a person going through a first nasty breakup might take longer to recover because he or she is sailing in such unfamiliar waters, or someone without a good network of support from family and friends might take longer than a more social person would, or an individual who suffers from an underlying condition like depression might find the process more drawn out than would someone with an inherently sunny disposition. Moreover, breakups born of betrayal can understandably demand extra time to get over.

Sometimes the grief and mourning over lost love are disproportionate to the intensity of the relationship, or to how long it actually went on. On one level this could be a variation on the Miss Havisham effect, as we saw back in part IV, or it could be because your fantasy about the relationship overtook the reality of it. Coming to terms with this common phenomenon requires being ruthless with oneself and forcing oneself to answer this question: Were my fantasies about our future together better than the reality of the time we actually shared?

To me one of the most interesting questions is whether or not we ever completely get over a really excruciating breakup. Sure, as time goes by we gradually withdraw our emotional investment, we move on and love other people, but the scar remains, perhaps not visible but still tender to the touch. And maybe on some level that's a good thing: The scar honors the attachment at its happiest.

Finally, I'd like to suggest that some part of us luxuriates in feeling the bad, bad, bad of heartbreak. There's something deeply affirming about the dirty hair, the detritus under the coffee table, and the "Are you okay?" phone calls, and I think that that something is self-knowledge. When all is said and done, we often look back on a period of heartbreak with something akin to pride, affection, and nostalgia, perhaps because we recognize that heartbreak is one of the most important states of being. There is satisfaction to be had, down the line, in knowing that we can be that dramatic and get through to the other side.

Horrid though it is, heartbreak is perhaps part of a larger order. I suspect that although those times of extreme pain, heartbreak's nadir, might be scattered in moments over the course of years, they are among the most important and transformative of our lives. Agony incubates empathy.

Additional Reading and Viewing

~

Nonfiction

Abelard, Pierre, and Heloise; Betty Radice, trans. *The Letters of Abelard and Heloise.* New York: Penguin, 2003.

Abelard, Pierre, and Heloise, William Levitan, trans. *Abelard and Heloise: The Letters and Other Writings.* Indianapolis, IN: Hackett Pub, 2007.

Ackerman, Diane. *A Natural History of Love,* New York: Vintage, 1995.

———, and Jeanne MacKin, eds. *The Book of Love.* New York: W. W. Norton, 1998.

Asendorf, Christoph, et al. *Edvard Munch: Theme and Variation.* Hamburg, Germany: Hatje Cantz Publishers, 2003.

Barash, David P., and Judith Eve Lipton. *The Myth of Monogamy: Fidelity and Infidelity in Animals and People.* New York: Holt, 2002.

Bainton, Roland H. *Here I Stand: A Life of Martin Luther.* New York: Abingdon-Cokesbury Press, 1950.

Brucker, Gene. *Giovanni and Lusanna: Love and Marriage in Renaissance Florence.* Berkeley: University of California Press, 1988.

Burge, James. *Heloise & Abelard.* London: Profile Books, 2003.

Coontz, Stephanie. *Marriage, a History: How Love Conquered Marriage.* New York: Penguin, 2005.

Dalrymple, William. *White Mughals: Love and Betrayal in Eighteenth-Century India.* London: HarperCollins, 2002.

Dearborn, Mary V. *Mailer: A Biography.* New York: Mariner, 2001.

Douglass, Paul. *Lady Caroline Lamb: A Biography.* New York: Palgrave MacMillan, 2004.

Dronke, Peter. *Women Writers of the Middle Ages: A Critical Study of Texts from Perpetua to Marguerite Porete.* Cambridge: Cambridge University Press, 1984.

Ettinger, Elżbieta. *Rosa Luxemburg: A Life.* Boston, MA: Beacon Press, 1986.

Evangelisti, Silvia. *Nuns: A History of Convent Life.* Oxford: Oxford University Press, 2007.

Faraone, Christopher. *Ancient Greek Love Magic.* Cambridge, MA: Harvard University Press, 2001.

Fisher, Helen. *Why We Love: The Nature and Chemistry of Romantic Love.* New York: Owl Books, 2004.

Foreman, Amanda. *Georgiana, Duchess of Devonshire.* New York: Modern Library, 2001.

Goddard, Simon. *Mozipedia: The Encyclopedia of Morrissey and the Smiths.* London: Ebury, 2009.

Hamon, Raeann R., and Bron B. Ingoldsby, eds. *Mate Selection Across Cultures.* Thousand Oaks, CA: SAGE Publications, 2003.

Hemingway, Mary Welsh. *How It Was.* New York: Alfred A. Knopf, 1976.

Jager, Eric. *The Book of the Heart.* Chicago: University of Chicago Press, 2000.

Kallir, Jane. *Egon Schiele: The Complete Works.* New York: Harry N. Abrams, 1998.

Kert, Bernice. *The Hemingway Women.* New York: W. W. Norton, 1998.

Kokoschka, Oskar; Olda Kokoschka and Alfred Marneau, eds. Mary Whittall trans. *Oskar Kokoschka: Letters 1905–1976.*

Kövecses, Zoltán. *Metaphor and Emotion: Language, Culture, and Body in Human Feeling.* Cambridge: Cambridge University Press, 2000.

———. *Emotion Concepts.* New York: Springer-Verlag, 1990.

Laven, Mary. *Virgins of Venice: Broken Vows and Cloistered Lives in the Renaissance Convent.* New York: Penguin, 2004.

Levine, Amir, and Rachel Heller. *Attached: The New Science of Adult Attachment and How It Can Help You Find—and Keep—Love.* New York: Tarcher, 2012.

Luxemburg, Rosa; Elżbieta Ettinger, trans. *Comrade and Lover: Rosa Luxemburg's Letters to Leo Jogiches.* Cambridge, MA: The MIT Press, 1979.

Mahon, Elizabeth Kerri. *Scandalous Women: The Lives and Loves of History's Most Notorious Women.* New York: Perigee, 2011.

Meade, Marion. *Eleanor of Aquitaine: A Biography.* New York: Hawthorn Books, 1977.

Mews, Constant J. *The Lost Love Letters of Heloise and Abelard: Perceptions of Dialogue in Twelfth-Century France.* New York: Palgrave Macmillan, 2008.

Owen, D. D. R. *Eleanor of Aquitaine: Queen and Legend.* Oxford: Blackwell, 1993.

Pernoud, Régine, Peter Wiles, trans. *Heloise and Abelard*. London: Collins, 1973.

Prideaux, Sue. *Edvard Munch: Behind the Scream*. New Haven, CT: Yale University Press, 2005.

Rollyson, Carl. *Rebecca West: A Life*. New York: Scribner, 1996.

Ruan, Fang Fu. *Sex in China: Studies in Sexology in Chinese Culture*. New York: Plenum Press, 1991.

Schröder, Klaus Albrecht, and Antonia Hoerschelmann, eds. *Edvard Munch: Theme and Variation*. Ostfildern-Ruit, Germany: Hatje Cantz, 2003.

Service, Shannon. "How to Mend a Broken Heart: Sifting Through Love's Smoldering Remains," in *Brink*, Berkeley: 2011.

Swafford, Jan. *Johannes Brahms: A Biography*. New York: Vintage, 1999.

Tomalin, Claire. *The Life and Death of Mary Wollstonecraft*. New York: Penguin, 1995.

van Dijken, Suzan. *John Bowlby: His Early Life*. London: Free Association Books, 1998.

Weidinger, Alfred. *Kokoschka and Alma Mahler*. New York: Prestel, 1996.

Young, Louisa. *The Book of the Heart*. New York: Doubleday, 2002.

Zaluski, Iwo, and Pamela Zaluski. *The Young Liszt*. London: Peter Owen, 1997.

Williams, Adrian, ed. *Portrait of Liszt: By Himself and His Contemporaries*. Oxford: Clarendon Press, 1990.

FICTION

Austen, Jane. *Sense and Sensibility*. New York: Penguin Classics, 2003.

Byatt, A. S. *Angels and Insects*. New York: Vintage, 1994.

Brontë, Emily. *Wuthering Heights*. New York: Signet Classics, 2011.

Dickens, Charles. *Great Expectations*. New York: Puffin, 2011.

Dunant, Sarah. *Sacred Hearts*. New York: Random House, 2009.

Eugenides, Jeffrey. *The Marriage Plot*. New York: Farrar, Straus and Giroux, 2011.

———. *Middlesex*. New York: Picador, 2007.

Fitzgerald, F. Scott. *The Great Gatsby*. New York: Scribner, 2004.

Flaubert, Gustav, and Lydia Davis, trans. *Madame Bovary*. New York: Penguin, 2010.

Frazier, Charles. *Cold Mountain*. New York: Atlantic Monthly Press, 1997.

Greene, Graham. *The End of the Affair*. New York: Penguin, 2004.

Hardy, Thomas. *Tess of the d'Urbervilles*. New York: Penguin Classics, 1999.

Hemingway, Ernest. *A Farewell to Arms*. New York: Scribner, 1995.

Hornby, Nick. *High Fidelity*. New York: Riverhead, 1996.

Ishiguro, Kazuo. *Never Let Me Go*. New York: Vintage, 2010.

James, Henry. *The Portrait of a Lady*. New York: Penguin Classics, 2003.

Maugham, W. Somerset. *The Painted Veil*. New York: Vintage, 2006.

McEwan, Ian. *Atonement*. New York: Anchor, 2003.

Murakami, Haruki, and Jay Rubin, trans. *Norwegian Wood*. New York: Vintage, 2000.

Nabokov, Vladimir. *Lolita*. New York: Vintage, 1989.

Ondaatje, Michael. *The English Patient*. New York: Vintage, 1993.

Schlink, Bernhard. *The Reader*. New York: Vintage, 2008.

Tolstoy, Leo. Constance Garnett, trans. *Anna Karenina*. Indianapolis, IN: Bobbs-Merrill Company, 1978.

———. *War and Peace*. New York: Vintage, 2008.

Waugh, Evelyn. *Brideshead Revisited*. New York: Back Bay, 1999.

Film

Tess (1979), with Nastassja Kinski.

Closer (2004), with Julia Roberts, Clive Owen, Natalie Portman, and Jude Law.

Dangerous Liaisons (1988), with Glenn Close, John Malkovich, Michelle Pfeiffer, and Uma Thurman.

Eternal Sunshine of the Spotless Mind (2004), with Jim Carrey and Kate Winslet.

High Fidelity (2000), with John Cusack and Iben Hjejle.

Impromptu (1991), with Judy Davis, Hugh Grant, Bernadette Peters, and Julian Sands.

Little Children (2006), with Kate Winslet.

Lost in Austen (2008), with Jemima Rooper and Hugh Bonneville.

Madame Bovary (1991), with Isabelle Huppert.

Never Let Me Go (2010), with Carey Mulligan, Andrew Garfield, and Keira Knightley.

The Painted Veil (2006), with Naomi Watts, Edward Norton, and Liev Schreiber.

Sense and Sensibility (1995), with Emma Thompson, Kate Winslet, Hugh Grant, and Alan Rickman.

Tess of the D'Urbervilles (1998), with Justine Waddell.